"Todd immediately turns the reader u
and language of faith. This is about, ir
sharing a set of beliefs'—yes, a warn
style, rich in personal examples, informative in research, and creates desire
to become more like Jesus in the twenty-first century."
Jo Anne Lyon, ambassador, general superintendent emerita,
The Wesleyan Church

"Is it possible some of the virtues we seek as followers of Jesus are actually
hindering our relationship with him and our witness to the world? In *The
Seven Deadly Virtues*, Todd Outcalt answers with a resounding yes! This book
is a must-read for all of us comfortable Christians who need to be made a
little less so."
Kurt Johnston, pastor to students, Saddleback Church

"The default response to problems, global or personal, is to bring out an
agreed-upon list of sins and link our failure with these sins. What if, instead
of our sins, our best practices got us to this undesirable place? In *The Seven
Deadly Virtues*, Todd Outcalt questions some of our most strongly held
virtues. Our commonly held list of virtues may be delivering unintended
consequences, be logically flawed, or even be unbiblical."
Bob Walters, author of *The Last Missionary*

"Leave it to Todd Outcalt and his gift of discernment to help us see the
shadow side of virtue. *The Seven Deadly Virtues* is for everyone who wants
to live beyond platitudes, values the road less taken, and isn't likely to
confuse the shine of brass for the luster of gold. A primer for mature people
of faith and all those who aspire to be."
Philip Gulley, Quaker pastor, author of *If the Church Were Christian*

"Could it be that virtues we've admired, like goodness and generosity, aren't
what God is actually seeking from us? Todd Outcalt, with clarity and
wisdom, shows us a more excellent way."
James C. Howell, senior pastor of Myers Park UMC, adjunct professor
of preaching, Duke Divinity School

The Seven Deadly Virtues

TEMPTATIONS IN OUR PURSUIT OF GOODNESS

TODD E. OUTCALT

IVP Books

An imprint of InterVarsity Press
Downers Grove, Illinois

InterVarsity Press
P.O. Box 1400, Downers Grove, IL 60515-1426
ivpress.com
email@ivpress.com

©2017 by Todd E. Outcalt

All rights reserved. No part of this book may be reproduced in any form without written permission from InterVarsity Press.

InterVarsity Press® is the book-publishing division of InterVarsity Christian Fellowship/USA®, a movement of students and faculty active on campus at hundreds of universities, colleges, and schools of nursing in the United States of America, and a member movement of the International Fellowship of Evangelical Students. For information about local and regional activities, visit intervarsity.org.

Scripture quotations, unless otherwise noted, are from the New Revised Standard Version of the Bible, copyright 1989 by the Division of Christian Education of the National Council of the Churches of Christ in the USA. Used by permission. All rights reserved.

While any stories in this book are true, some names and identifying information may have been changed to protect the privacy of individuals.

Cover design: Faceout Studio
Interior design: Dan van Loon

ISBN 978-0-8308-4476-0 (print)
ISBN 978-0-8308-8100-0 (digital)

Printed in the United States of America ♾

As a member of the Green Press Initiative, InterVarsity Press is committed to protecting the environment and to the responsible use of natural resources. To learn more, visit greenpressinitiative.org.

Library of Congress Cataloging-in-Publication Data
Names: Outcalt, Todd, author.
Title: The seven deadly virtues : temptations in our pursuit of goodness /
   Todd E. Outcalt.
Description: Downers Grove : InterVarsity Press, 2017. | Includes
   bibliographical references.
Identifiers: LCCN 2016046960 (print) | LCCN 2016052037 (ebook) | ISBN
   9780830844760 (pbk. : alk. paper) | ISBN 9780830881000 (eBook)
Subjects: LCSH: Virtues. | Temptation.
Classification: LCC BV4630 .O98 2017 (print) | LCC BV4630 (ebook) | DDC
   241/.4--dc23
LC record available at https://lccn.loc.gov/2016046960

P 25 24 23 22 21 20 19 18 17 16 15 14 13 12 11 10 9 8 7 6 5 4 3 2 1

Y 34 33 32 31 30 29 28 27 26 25 24 23 22 21 20 19 18 17

To Paula

CONTENTS

Two rabbis were debating virtues. One rabbi asked,
"And what is a virtue?" The other answered,
"A virtue is timeless and unchanging." But the first rabbi said,
"I must tell you story."

There was a beautiful bird that lived its entire life inside a luxurious
cage. One day another bird flew into the cage when the master
of the house had inadvertently left the cage door open.
The second bird said to the first,
"Why don't you fly away with me to freedom?"

But the beautiful bird answered, "I know nothing of
the freedom of which you speak. Each day I receive meals
from my master's hand. My domicile is cleaned. I am secure
and happy. Life is good. And whenever
I see my reflection in the mirror, I sing."

"But you are a prisoner," said the second bird.

"I think not," said the beautiful bird.
"How can one be a prisoner while enjoying all of this?"

At that word the second bird flew away to freedom while
the beautiful bird remained happy and singing in its cage,
unsuspecting of its true condition.

BASED ON A JEWISH PARABLE

Two looked out from the prison bars,
One saw mud, the other stars.

TRADITIONAL SAYING

Be careful not to practice your righteousness
in front of others to be seen by them.

MATTHEW 6:1 NIV

INTRODUCTION

Where virtue is, there are many snares.

St. John Chrysostom

Choose your enemies carefully . . .
for you will become like them.

Ancient Proverb

IN CLASSIC CHRISTIAN THEOLOGY THE CHURCH has long taught and preached against the "seven deadly sins," which are traditionally defined as wrath, greed, sloth, pride, lust, envy, and gluttony. Theologians have addressed these sins from many angles, whole books have been written about them, and most pastors have addressed them at one time or another. In fact, these sins are so prominent, so well pronounced, that it is difficult to miss them. These sins can eat away at our relationships, our work, our homes, and our interior (or spiritual) lives.

But these same truths also hold up when we examine our virtues, which may be described for our purposes here as those values and loves that we cherish dearly and that we often believe are shaping our faith and our futures.

As St. John Chrysostom once noted centuries ago, our virtues are as problematic as our sins. It's just that our virtues are far more cleverly disguised and have a tendency to embolden us with the sin of pride, which is difficult to identify in the life of faith. The Christian faith has always contained these tensions. While virtues are often regarded as the goal of faith (to be better people, to be holy) these virtues can also erode our faith in God if we are not careful. Our virtues can become our pride and joy—those great achievements we have obtained, those accomplishments that set us apart from "sinful" masses who have not yet ascended to the pinnacle of faith. We can even cherish these virtues over God (which is idolatry). Often, our virtues are what land us in trouble. Our virtues can even be in opposition to the gospel.

No doubt some will be troubled by this assertion. (We often want to protect our virtues and hold them up to the light as truth.) Others may dismiss the idea of deadly virtues.

Regardless, I hope readers of good faith will at least undertake this adventure of exploring Christianity from the vantage point of virtues rather than sins. Instead of observing the Christian life from the underside, we may find equally troubling difficulties from the topside. We may also discover that the Christian faith, as often presented and cherished, has the potential to hide a multitude of deadly virtues. We may discover that some of our most cherished assumptions about faith are being destroyed by our virtues rather than our sins.

Parables of Virtue

Most of the time, when the parables of Jesus are discussed or parsed, the takeaway is that the parables address certain sins or those debased attitudes that Jesus wanted to address.

For example, the parable of the sower (Lk 8:4-15) is often regarded as a parable about various levels of faith—with the good soil representing, of course, people of strong faith and character. But within the context and the audience who were first listening to this parable, we can see an entirely different outcome. In the explanation that Jesus provides (vv. 11-15) we can see that the types of soils do not represent those who don't believe but those who claim they do. Misplaced faith, myopic faith, lip-service faith—that is what the parable is about. The parable essentially asks a question: Do we regard faith as something we possess, or does faith possess us? The differences are noteworthy. It is the difference between faith as a noun and faith as a verb, between regarding faith as a possession and regarding faith as an action that produces fruitfulness and endurance (v. 15).

The parable of the laborers (Mt 20:1-16) is another story commonly misconstrued. Jesus told this parable to demonstrate that "the last will be first, and the first will be last." In other words, we must always be on the lookout for our virtues—such as valuing our faithfulness, perseverance, and unchanging beliefs over God's grace and hospitality. These were the attitudes that the early laborers of the parable possessed; they could not accept God's generosity and equal reward for the latecomers. How often do we see these very attitudes at play in congregations where new people have no voice or where longtime members regard their history and understanding as superior to that of the young? This is a parable about misplaced attitudes of the faithful.

Likewise, the parable of the prodigal son (Lk 15:11-32) is most frequently used as a springboard to talk about salvation or to illustrate how people can squander their lives through their own desires and devices. Often the parable is regarded as a salvation story, with the wayward young man being welcomed home (to heaven) by the loving Father. But we can miss the attitude of the older son, which is what the parable is really about. Within the context and the audience that Jesus was speaking to, this parable is principally designed to speak to the misplaced virtues of goodness, holiness, and faithfulness that the religious leaders of Jesus day believed they possessed, virtues that made them better than the lowly prodigals. But this is a grace parable, and the story invites the faithful to see themselves as the older son, who cannot accept the generosity of almighty God. It is not a parable of virtue but a parable of change.

Parsing other parables in this way, it is amazing to note how often Jesus was speaking to the religious people instead of "sinners." The parables are most frequently addressing deadly virtues rather than deadly sins. As such, the parables have a great power to speak to the foibles and failures of the faithful. The parables rarely address those outside the household of faith but instead challenge our sensibilities and values, those beliefs we hold so sacred and so dear, but that can actually become a barrier to God.

Whenever Jesus spoke about salvation, he did so in the hope of transforming religious people most of all. Salvation is about having our virtues transformed and rightly placed, as well as our sins.

Looking Within

There is a wonderful parable about a father and son who set out on a journey. As they prepared for this adventure, the son noticed that the father placed a small pebble inside his shoe before they set out. "Father," the son asked, "why are you placing a pebble inside your shoe?" The father answered, "I need to be reminded of the difficulties of others. So every time I take a step, I feel some discomfort. It is not good to walk through life without an awareness of life's hardships."

In many respects the teachings of Jesus are like pebbles in the shoes of the faithful. Focusing on our virtues rather than our sins affords us the opportunity to remember that discipleship is never easy (nor was it meant to be). Rather, discipleship is difficult, even demanding. Awareness of ourselves and others is required.

Dealing with our deadly virtues also requires, as Jesus said, new ears to hear and new eyes to see. Throughout church history a changing array of virtues have hindered the church. Some of these cherished virtues, in fact, gave rise to both tremendous horrors (such as pogroms or the crusades) as well as changes (such as reformation, repentance, or revival).

Virtues, of course, are not in and of themselves bad. Virtues are important and can be life giving.

But virtues—misunderstood, misapplied, or misused—can become barriers too. Virtues, when seen as an ultimate end or as principles that give us privilege or power, or that we protect for ourselves, can produce deadly outcomes. Virtues all too frequently masquerade as the ultimate goal of the Christian life.

As St. John Chrysostom once observed, "Where virtue is, there are many snares."[1] And indeed there are. The Scriptures are replete with the same observation. Sometimes it is not our sins and weaknesses that hold us back from serving God but the values we elevate above God. And as many ancient voices and prophets have indicated, we often accept our sins and are blinded by the virtues that produce them. Jesus observed these deadly virtues in the religious of his day, and we can be certain that these, and a host of others, are equally present in the establishments and attitudes of our time. But we while we can confess our sins, what do we do with our deadly virtues?

John Scotus, an Irish theologian and poet of the ninth century, once wrote, "No vice is found but within the shadow of some virtue."[2]

These are difficult truths to accept. But they are necessary if we are to embrace the abundant life that Jesus talked about.

Jesus affirmed we could experience new life, a salvation that would embrace us now and in the life to come. Even the faithful can find it. But we first have to let go of our virtues. We have to be willing to come out of the shadow of our virtues and into the light.

KEEPING YOUR FAITH
WITHOUT DESTROYING
THE FAITH OF OTHERS

Beware of practicing your piety before
others in order to be seen by them.

MATTHEW 6:1

YEARS AGO, AFTER PRAYING WITH A DYING WOMAN in a hospital ward, I was blindsided by one of the nurses who had been attending to her. This nurse asked me to step into a vacant room and began to pepper me with theological questions: *What did I believe about salvation? Did I believe in an everlasting hell? Did I believe that we were living in the end times? How did I know that I was saved?*

At first I thought this nurse was seeking answers or had genuine questions about the Christian faith. However, in time I became aware that she was not a seeker but was administering a test to see if I qualified as a true believer. The more questions she asked, and the more I tried to give satisfactory answers to her questions, the more apparent it became that I was flunking her exam. In the end she brandished a small, trifold tract from her smock and demanded that I read it. She also invited me to attend her church, where I would be exposed to the "true faith" and "hear the one true Word."

I was saddened by this woman's narrow understanding of faith—a set of beliefs that held her captive in a tiny world of hostility and judgment. Everyone she met was a potential enemy of God, or at best a potential convert to her "true" understanding of faith.

No doubt there were many others who had encountered this nurse and had based their opinion of Christians, Christianity, or even the church on her approach to the faith. She had become adept at "sharing" her faith, but toward what ends? And I have wondered since how often she has given Jesus a black eye through her zeal.

No doubt this woman was a Christian. Like me, she believed in the good news of Jesus Christ and zealously shared this news with others. In fact, she inadvertently challenged me to take a step back, to look at my professed faith in Jesus, and to make adjustments in my attitude or approach. *What beliefs were guiding my life? How was I sharing the good news of Jesus? Where, ultimately, was my trust?*

Over the years I have learned that few Christians share *all* beliefs in common. Despite what some teach about "one faith," "one unchanging gospel," or "the eternal truth," Christians have always differed in their understandings of Christ, in the nature and ministry of the church, and in their respective doctrines. The early church was diverse in belief and practice. People talked about Jesus in different ways—as evidenced by the fact that there are four Gospels *and* various epistles. While the core of the Christian message was the same, there were different expressions of the faith and practice. It would be helpful to keep these distinctions in mind as we explore the faith Jesus seemed to describe.

For certain, most Christians operate with a set of beliefs— traditions, perhaps, but sometimes clearly defined doctrines or ideas about God that have sustained them or their communities for centuries. And while the faith of many grows and changes over time, it has a tendency to become a set of rules, a litmus test that clearly shows who is in and out, or even a series of affirmations that comfort those who hold them but trouble those who don't.

In essence, faith as *belief* can be a problem, and Jesus warned his disciples to beware faith's dark side: the allure of self-righteousness, the adherence to unyielding rules, demonstrations of hatred in the name of witness, and the subtle self-serving ends faith can lead to. In fact, Jesus warned us about *ourselves* and what we might build in the name of faith.

Many will balk at the suggestion that faith could be a deadly virtue. After all, isn't Christianity centered in faith? Doesn't the Bible—and especially Jesus—speak of faith as the ultimate virtue? Aren't we striving for more faith instead of less? Shouldn't we desire strong faith, vibrant faith, faith that can be shared with others in word and deed?

Absolutely!

Then again, not so fast.

Scripture also speaks of the consequences of misplaced faith, of faith that, even if well meaning, can destroy our relationship with others and even lead us to destruction and death. The Bible provides dozens (perhaps hundreds) of examples that show how faithful zeal and myopic faithfulness to our concepts and understandings of God often lead to less-than-faithful ends.

It is not difficult to see the vestiges of misplaced faith today. Many equate the Christian faith with the pathway to success or lift up faith in Jesus like a talisman in order to gain votes, security, or prestige. At first blush it may seem that Christian faith is a wonderful thing—like a commodity to barter—but as we listen to the teachings of Christ we discover that faith is fraught with difficulties and sacrifices.

And in our time—when television and media serve as attractive cousins of Christian proclamation—it is easy for our faith to fall prey to easy answers, slick slogans, or even clichés. The church must continually be on guard.

Jesus asked his followers to beware practicing their faith as a show. And when Jesus sent his disciples into the fields for the harvest, he also warned them of many false and destructive mindsets. In essence he warned them to be aware of themselves and their attitudes. He called them to share faith evidenced by love, to helping neighbors, and to ministries of hope and healing. While it is true that Jesus asked his disciples, "Who do you say that I am?" he also asked them to live in faith as an expression of loving God and neighbor. Consider this short list of instructions.

- Unless you change and become like children, you will never enter the kingdom of heaven. (Mt 18:3)

- The harvest is plentiful but the workers are few. Ask the Lord of the harvest, therefore, to send out workers into his harvest field. (Mt 9:37-38 NIV)

- Do not judge, or you too will be judged. (Mt 7:1 NIV)

- As you go, proclaim the good news, "The kingdom of heaven has come near." Cure the sick, raise the dead, cleanse the lepers, cast out demons. You received without payment; give without payment. (Mt 10:7-8)

- If any want to become my followers, let them deny themselves and take up their cross and follow me. (Mk 8:34)

Even a cursory exploration of Jesus' teachings reveal that he taught his followers to focus on living their faith rather than sharing a set of beliefs. Christ defined faith in terms of a movement of God, not as an assent to a set of beliefs. For Jesus, faith was a verb, not a noun. Faith was action moved by love, generosity, self-sacrifice, and looking to the needs of others.

Recently, in a letter addressed to an Italian journalist, Pope Francis said, "Truth, according to the Christian faith, is God's love for us in Jesus Christ. Therefore, truth is a relationship."[1]

As Pope Francis noted, the Christian faith—the gospel—is more about relationship, how Christ's followers embody love, than it is assent to beliefs. When Jesus talked about following him, he noted the importance of "going," "giving," "healing," "proclaiming," and "following." These are relational and active.

Faith is living the gospel, the good news of salvation through Christ, in word and deed. Nowhere in the Gospels do we encounter Jesus describing faith as merely a set of beliefs or doctrines. Faith was not a virtue to be exploited or reproduced through coercion or power. Rather, humility, simplicity, helpfulness, love, and service were the defining features of the faith Jesus described.

Christians have always been called to embody the love of Jesus, to proclaim the salvation that he has made for us through his death and resurrection. And while these beliefs are most certainly creedal and doctrinal, the goal of faith is Christ himself, placing our full confidence in his salvation received by grace through faith.

And yet it is easy for us to set our faith on a pedestal, to draw attention to ourselves and how *much* we believe (and *what* we believe) rather than demonstrating faith through acts of service and generosity.

I know that I am often guilty of viewing faith as the former rather than the latter. That is why faith is not always a virtue. In fact, faith that draws attention to ourselves can lead us away from God. Faith that draws attention to ourselves does not draw us closer to Jesus.

One example comes from my own Methodist tradition. When John Wesley was preaching in eighteenth-century England, many well-meaning people of faith took exception to his message and methods. Wesley noted that the faith of many had become "a dimly-burning wick." Child labor was rampant throughout England; the slave trade was proliferating throughout England and the American colonies; and the poor, the lonely, and prisoners were being ignored by the church. Wesley sought change. He desired deep faith to be wrought in the human heart. Wesley noted that the faith of many was no longer a life-giving grace but a deadly virtue. Faith had become belief rather than the love of Christ moved to action.

Many of the clergy of Wesley's time wouldn't allow him to preach from their pulpits. At times church mobs—intending to protect their turf and honor the traditions of the Church of England—became loud and boisterous, sometimes driving away those who had come "in the name of the Lord" to speak good news to the poor, the outcast, or the disenfranchised.

Today too our "faithful" practices can lead to exclusion and judgment. Pastors like me, for example, can be quick to defend a particular belief system, a set of creeds or traditions and practices that does little more than make us feel good about "faith" while ignoring the needs of the world. Whenever this happens faith can become, as the prophet Micah once noted, an empty, rote expression.

> [God] has told you, O mortal, what is good;
> and what does the LORD require of you
> but to do justice, and to love kindness,
> and to walk humbly with your God? (Mic 6:8)

Jesus frequently addressed these prophetic expressions, these tendencies we all have to find a misplaced virtue in faith. He even experienced these temptations himself. In the Gospel of Luke, Jesus begins his ministry by first retreating to the desert to be tempted by the devil (Lk 4:1-13). When the temptations come, the devil does not tempt Jesus with obvious vices (such as lust or pride), but with the very powers and virtues that Jesus possesses.

Because Jesus is hungry, the devil challenges him to use his faith to turn stones into bread. "If you are really God's Son, then exercise your faith to meet your own need!" (v. 3, my paraphrase). Here we see the virtue of faith being used as a temptation. The idea that faith somehow provokes God to give us anything we want is a temptation for us too. How often have we heard clichés such as "Name it and claim it!" or "Believe it and receive it!" or "God rewards you in accordance with your faith."

But Jesus doesn't fall for these false concepts of faith. Rather, he retreats to a deep faith that holds to complete trust in God, regardless of his situation or personal need: "A person does not live by bread only, but by every word that precedes from God."

In the temptations of Jesus we also encounter the gospel. We see what Jesus has overcome on our behalf. We see that faith is not to be exploited for our own needs. Faith is not to be treated as a commodity, the means of exchange we use to barter with the almighty. Rather, we can trust that Christ has overcome. He has already won the victory—and we need not use faith to draw attention to ourselves or our own desires.

Beginner's Faith

It is helpful for us to remember that faith is, in essence, the gospel, which is hope and trust in Christ for our joy and salvation. Faith is not an end in itself. The end of faith is Jesus. In other words, faith points us to God, who is our salvation, life, and hope. Faith is not a commodity we use to hurt or belittle others. In fact, Jesus warned his followers about making such judgments lest they forget their own weaknesses. Faith leads to humility and a secure trust in the Creator and Redeemer of the universe. Faith leads us to relationship—an awareness of God's presence with us—and to the supreme joy of loving God and serving others.

Jesus addressed misplaced faith, saying, "Beware of practicing your piety before others in order to be seen by them; for then you have no reward from your Father in heaven" (Mt 6:1).

As a pastor, I have caught myself making judgments about others based on their "weak" faith. I have caught myself asking questions like: *Why don't these people pray more? Why don't they give more? Why don't they attend worship more often? Where is their faith?*

It's easy to slip into the pharisaical attitude Jesus encountered among some of the religious leaders of his day. In our zeal to make our faith strong, active, and visible, we often are enamored with faith itself. Jesus warns us of this type of misplaced faith, which is more akin to self-righteousness or faith for faith's sake than the humble, cooperative faith (complete trust in his grace) Jesus desires for his disciples.

But self-righteousness doesn't redeem us. Fear doesn't lead to faith. We often fall into the snare of protecting our faith (or our turf) instead of standing on the grace and salvation of Jesus.

I struggle in the awareness of my own weaknesses, and realize that when I am trying to follow Jesus, faith as a set of beliefs can become most confusing. I need to stay focused on Jesus in order to be faithful to him! This means I need his strength if I am to share his love instead of my fear.

This is not the only way the church struggles with faith.

Today, American culture is littered with ideas about the Christian faith that are more akin

> IN OUR ZEAL TO MAKE OUR FAITH STRONG, ACTIVE, AND VISIBLE, WE OFTEN ARE ENAMORED WITH FAITH ITSELF.

to winning a prizefight than to serving humanity with humility and generosity. We can hardly listen to religious television or radio without being swept up in political language, with words like *liberal* and *conservative* far more in vogue than words like *service, give, pray, blessed,* or *joy*—words that Jesus used to describe the attitudes and work that would set his followers apart in the world. In the marketplace of ideas Christianity often falls into the winner and loser mindset when church leaders vie to crush other denominations, traditions, or voices. The American church seems to agree on very little these days.

Today, even our political debates are peppered with confessions of belief. Many politicians have espoused Christianity in order to gain votes or popularity. And many Christians buy into these hollow proclamations instead of remembering the words of Jesus: "My kingdom is not of this world." Living the Christian faith has become more difficult in this media-saturated age. Soundbites and clichés can be more appealing than deep conversations in the church. Christians on various sides of any debate now speak about the faith being "hijacked" or "dumbed down."

But we don't have to stand on a political dais in order to see how faith can become self-serving or self-promoting. And we don't have to be great theologians to see how easily Christians can fall into ideological camps rather than falling in love with Jesus and being moved by his love.

When our congregation sent a team of people to serve in Haiti, I encountered these self-serving ideas of faith. Soon after our team departed, one lady in our congregation pointed out that there were "needy people in our own community" and that "we don't need to travel abroad to proclaim the gospel"—implying that we didn't need to send people to another country but should stay at home and minister to "our own." There is some truth in what she said. The needy are at our own backdoors. But her contention was that faith should stay close to home and that proclaiming the gospel was a personal source of comfort.

On another occasion, while traveling with a mission team to Guatemala, our team encountered another Christian mission team in the airport when we arrived. This group sported brightly colored T-shirts that read "Bringing Christ to Guatemala." Although well-meaning, I wondered what the Christian communities in Guatemala would think of the implied message. Was this group really the first to bring Christ to Guatemala? Hadn't Christ and his church been in Guatemala for hundreds of years before this group's arrival? Did the group come to share *the faith* or were they there to follow Jesus, to live the gospel of giving as well as receiving?

Faith is difficult to live out. We tend to place ourselves at the head of the faith train. It's tempting to draw attention to ourselves rather than to Christ. We often proclaim and live a gospel other than that of Christ's redemption and hope for the world.

As far as faith is concerned, we are always beginners. In fact, humility, uncertainty, repentance, joy, and devotion offer us a much richer and deeper faith than we can discover in arrogance, certainty, rules, judgment, or the many types of self-directed spirituality so prevalent today. Unfortunately, we more often encounter the latter type of faith in ourselves and in the church. Once we believe we have all the truth, there is no place left for God to work in the dusty corners of our lives. Would we need God's grace and forgiveness any longer if we possessed all truth? Do we need God's love and presence to help us in our sufferings if we have a faith that can remove these distractions via a simple prayer?

As one pastoral colleague noted, Christians have a tendency to reduce faith to a set of clichés or platitudes. Perhaps we have all been guilty of speaking of the faith in formulaic terms—as if prayer were magic—or by giving the impression that God responds to us and makes everything right if we only believe. It is easy to make our set of beliefs and platitudes the end of faith rather than finding our alpha and omega in Jesus and his redemption.

While attending a national pastors' conference some years ago, a presenter made some bold claims. This pastor (actually a well-recognized televangelist) related a story about his experience at the airport. "When I arrived this morning," he told us, "I discovered that my luggage had been lost. But I knelt and prayed right there in the airport, by the luggage turnstiles, and when I looked up, I found that my suitcase was there in front of me."

As he continued relating this story of faith, I could see that others were uncomfortable—even disbelieving. He closed by telling us, "God continues to show me that we can do all things through Christ, that any mountain can be moved if we only believe. When we don't get the results we want, friends, we simply don't have enough faith—we have not put our whole confidence in God."

Afterward, another pastor said to me, "No wonder so many people reject the Christian faith outright or feel that faith is a sham. When prayer is reduced to magic, or when God answers a prayer for luggage but can't fix cancer or bring peace or reduce human suffering, we are telling people that God is only concerned about trivial things. We reduce God to a servant of the meaningless."

I had to agree with this friend. Over the years I have heard many well-meaning people affirm similar platitudes and clichés, holding God up as Lord of the luggage instead of Lord of life. But rarely do these folks peek behind the curtain of faith to see how trivial their prayers can be. If we can pray for (and receive) answers in the form of restored luggage, repaired tires, or broken toys, then why can't God answer the more significant prayers related to restored relationships, repaired marriages, or broken lives?

> THE GOSPEL IS ABOUT CHRIST'S COMPLETED WORK OF SALVATION, NOT PRAYERS THAT PROVOKE GOD TO GIVE US OUR DESIRES.

This kind of faith rarely stops to ponder the significance of these questions, but they are essential to ask if we are to restore the meaning of the gospel and keep faith from becoming a deadly virtue. The gospel is about Christ's completed work of salvation, not prayers that provoke God to give us our desires.

The faith that Jesus describes is anything but trivial. Christian faith, as Jesus describes it, always leads to humility, always points us to his love, his salvation, his death and resurrection on our behalf. Faith also leads to questions. Faith is needed because there *is* struggle, not because we have removed all struggles from our lives.

In fact, this is the significance of the creeds, which have been proclaimed throughout the centuries. We need to be reminded of the faith without which the church cannot live faithfully. This faith—this gospel—cannot be reduced to traditionalism, which has often been described as "the dead faith of the living." Rather, we look to tradition, to proper doctrine and teaching, as "the living faith of the dead." This is an important distinction for our time. Perhaps especially for a time such as this.

The church dares not fall away from the gospel—the good news of Jesus and his salvation. This is the faith that makes us alive in him! And we are called to share Jesus with others in word and deed.

Many people are frustrated with the church and faith. This is especially true of younger people, who are not looking to the church for platitudes and rules, but for authenticity and integrity. Many younger people have positive thoughts about Jesus, but negative thoughts about the church. Likewise, they have positive thoughts about following Jesus, but negative thoughts about the people who claim faith in Jesus.

Perhaps this is why the new atheism is so much in vogue today—especially in America. It's far easier for people to serve humanity without God than it is to believe in a God who offers us a long list of rules to follow. A recent Barna study revealed that a high percentage of younger Americans see Christians as hypocritical, angry, homophobic, or overtly political. How remarkable it would it be if people equated Christians with love, kindness, helpfulness, acceptance, and joy! What if, instead of Christians being regarded as antiscience or antimodern, Christians were regarded as thoughtful or caring?

The church is not called to forsake creeds or doctrinal affirmations, but to bring these beliefs to life in the good news. Our various beliefs and traditions about Jesus should be living affirmations, not dead platitudes. At the end of the day the gospel is what makes Christ known to the world and brings hope and salvation. *We* are not the way—Christ is.

But why is this gospel so difficult? Why does the church often travel so far afield of Christ's teachings about humble faith, about searching, about joy, about asking questions and living in grace?

Jesus told many stories about being lost and found—about searching for and finding God in unexpected places. A lost coin, a lost sheep, a lost son (Lk 15)—these parables point us to a faith that is more akin to seeking than finding, more suited to humility than certainty, born more of love and hospitality than narrow-mindedness and sectarianism.

But something in human nature loves rules and a ruler. We feel compelled—not only in school, sports, and business, but also in the church—to measure ourselves against others and to enforce rules that make us feel more secure. We want to know how we stack up. And often we want to make sure we measure up to or surpass others when it comes to keeping the rules. Sadly, over time, these very rules and sets of beliefs are often equated with faith—and that is when faith can become a deadly virtue, the type of faith that Jesus warned against.

These themes—law versus grace, legalism versus love, freedom versus gospel—have been explored throughout Christian history. Movements such as Catholic orders and monasticism have come from them. And reformations, renewals, and revivals have refreshed faith with Christ's call rather than remaining in dead forms of belief. Regardless of our church traditions, all can point to historic moments of refreshment when the gospel came alive again. And we long for them today.

Indeed, something happens to us—and to the church—when our faith becomes a dead thing instead of a living gospel. Often, in our well-meaning attempts to keep the church holy or satisfying or even spirited, we lose our ability to welcome the stranger or to embrace the poor, the hurt, and the dying. Our communities become hotbeds of self-centered and self-righteous individuals who no longer have a simple, life-giving faith. I don't say this as an indictment against others but as a reminder to myself to keep faith God-centered, to keep faith humble. Faith should not be *me* directed but *other* directed. Christian faith is the good news birthed and crucified and raised in Jesus of Nazareth.

We should never allow faith in God to become a set of rules or a self-centered exercise that has more to do with personal growth or self-fulfillment than the gospel of Jesus. Faith should never be equated with something we coerce *from God* but should be regarded as a loving relationship *with God*. These are difficult observations to make, especially when I see these deficiencies and this misplaced faith within myself.

But perhaps the church has always struggled with these realities.

These are tough times, and they require deep thought by all people of faith. In our time there are many threats against the church. Secularism and apathy are two examples. And shallowness and clichés do not serve us well. Faith, as Jesus described it, is a way forward. When the church is defined as those who love Jesus and share his love with others, we become a gospel people.

Many people in our society have given up on organized religion. They see all faith communities as inclined to hate, fear, and violence. Some see all religion as a horrible and threatening movement that is destroying the world.

Because of this, it is imperative that Christians embrace the humble path described by Jesus. True Christian faith does not produce or spread fear. It does not try to annihilate other religions. Nor does it acquiesce to the idea that all religions are the same. Rather faith, as described by Jesus, is a journey of love and humility and service. Christian faith looks to Jesus, the pioneer and perfecter of faith, who makes all things new and calls us to bold service, not to fear or temerity.

We moderns are not immune to misplaced faith. In fact, we may be all the more prone to make faith a virtue, especially when difficult times pull us toward easy answers, toward the loudest voices, or toward the notion that we must return to a golden age of faith. Today we also feel the pull of hatred and violence as the answer to the world's ills. You might think that those who follow the prince of peace would reject violence, yet many church leaders are hard-pressed to find peace-minded people in the pews.

Today, faith is more often associated with game-winning touchdowns, flush bank accounts, personal achievement, and good health than it is with preaching good news to the poor, clothing the naked, healing the sick, or visiting the imprisoned (Lk 4:18-19). We are more likely to hear sermons about faith that can move mountains of cash than about moving mountains for social change. We are more likely to think of faith as personal rather than communal, as individual and heavenly rather than corporate or immanent. And we are more likely to think of the church as a *place* rather than as a *community* of gracious people. Many people in the church are far more likely to ask, "What can the church do for me?" than, "What can I do for others?"

These are not insignificant differences but are at the very heart of the dichotomy between gospel faith and faith as a deadly virtue.

Mature Faith

The goal of the Christian life is to know Jesus and to share his love with others. Faith for faith's sake, for tradition's sake, or for denomination's sake does not ultimately give us life. The writer of Hebrews admonishes the faithful to press on toward maturity (Heb 6:1). And the apostle Paul asks the Corinthians to grow up and begin eating solid food rather than being satisfied with infants' milk (1 Cor 3:2).

A mature faith has come of age and can rest in the security of God's love and grace. Faith that constantly defends, fortifies, or berates does not exemplify the simple trust Christ calls us to. Most of the interactions Jesus had with the faithful people of his time pitted the defenders of the faith against the generosity and hospitality Jesus offered to others. We cannot forget that Jesus was often accused of associating with "sinners." But Jesus demonstrated what faith looks like: ultimate trust and righteous living that would lead to the cross.

The apostle Paul describes Christ's faith:

Let the same mind be in you that was in Christ Jesus,
    who, though he was in the form of God,
        did not regard equality with God
        as something to be exploited,
    but emptied himself,
        taking the form of a slave,
        being born in human likeness.
    And being found in human form,
        he humbled himself
        and became obedient to the point of death—
        even death on a cross. (Phil 2:5-8)

What a remarkable faith—and how difficult it is for us to grasp! Most of us struggle mightily to trust in the gospel fortified by historic creeds and sought through biblical discourse and study. We often struggle to live our faith *in Jesus*, much preferring to believe things *about Jesus*.

Some years ago a young lady named Susie helped me grasp this more fully. Susie, an autistic teenager who was very active in our youth group, had difficulty participating in the deeper discussions about the Bible or prayer. But Susie was a servant, and her gentle and simple faith was an inspiration to everyone in the church. Although Susie could not express the historical creeds of the church or discuss theology, she had a deep faith in Jesus.

SOMETHING WONDERFUL HAPPENS WHEN WE NO LONGER NEED TO DEFEND OUR FAITH, WEIGH IT AGAINST ANOTHER'S FAITH, OR HOLD OUR FAITH UP TO THE LIGHT TO BE ADMIRED.

One summer during a mission trip, everyone was asked to express why they had decided to participate in helping others and what they hoped to bring to the mission. Most of the participants—myself included—attempted to give reasons for our generosity or offer evidences of our various gifts and abilities. We talked about what we were bringing rather than what God was giving. But Susie expressed it best: "I just love Jesus and I want show it."

There was nothing self-centered or self-absorbed—no vice—in Susie's faith. Her faith was so gentle, so outward, and so life giving it changed the flavor of our mission trip and made everyone aware of our limitations and our need to trust Christ.

Something wonderful happens when we no longer need to defend our faith, weigh it against another's faith, or hold our faith up to the light to be admired. We can share faith that is genuine and born of a grace-filled experience with Christ.

God knows, we don't need faith to be a deadly virtue. We have enough vices to overcome. Our faith should be focused on the God who loves us, who calls us to serve, and who has redeemed the world.

Faith Imperfect

Perhaps our greatest challenge in faith is faith itself. More precisely: we can grow in faith only when we recognize that our faith is imperfect. There is always more to know, more to learn, more to do. When we think we have arrived at faith, our faith goes awry.

We should not be confused by this. Everyone described in the Scriptures was imperfect in faith too. The Bible is honest in that way. Scripture does not offer us glimpses of perfect people living "holy" lives, but people like us struggling with questions and doubts, but pressing on toward God's call.

Hebrews 11 offers a revealing roll call of the faithful. In it we read about Abraham and Joseph and Moses—individuals with various weaknesses, vices, and doubts. But they are called faithful nonetheless. The list also includes an odd assortment of dubious characters: Rahab (prostitute), Samson (womanizer), Jephthah (violent), and David (adulterer).

These are not bright stars but dimly burning wicks. But in the end, they reveal that faithfulness is not so much about rule keeping or right living as it is about God's gifts and grace. People are imperfect, and our faith is too. We aren't after our righteousness but God's. We aren't called to look for our own solutions but God's redemption.

Faith is often associated with certainty. To express doubt or uncertainty is deemed a sign of weakness. God forbid that people of faith change their minds. Faith can be unyielding, uncooperative, and even uncompromising. Instead of seeking God through service or hospitality, people of faith tend to hole up in their respective tribes, wall themselves off from the world, and proclaim their "faith" as the one truth.

A friend recently told me that his long-held beliefs had been shattered. "What happened?" I asked. He explained that he had attended a class to learn more about the history of his Christian faith tradition, and became disappointed by the attitude of the teacher. "I guess the last straw for me was when the leader told me that everyone who was not a part of our faith was going to hell. But I know so many people who hold to other beliefs and yet live out their faith by helping the poor, the sick, the needy. The theology in the class just didn't make sense to me."

Hearing my friend's story, I was overcome with sadness. I felt his pain and hoped I hadn't used faith as a sledgehammer to beat people down. I want to share good news with others, not bad news and condemnation.

As I grow older and learn that I am weak and broken and stand in need of God's grace, I feel the weight of faith as a deadly virtue. I have far more questions than answers, and I am still going on to salvation (as the Scriptures describe it). I have grown, I hope, in my ability to embrace others in their diversity of belief and practice, and to see the image of God in those who are quite different from me. This approach to faith has given me more life, joy, and hope.

Once, standing over the grave of a fellow believer who had lived a life of humility and service, I listened as others described him as a "man of few words" and "a servant of God." Many expressed their respect for this man because of his actions, not because of his beliefs. Others noted how his faith had led him to care for others. And when his son read from the Bible, he chose a telling portion from the book of James. "[Faith] that is pure and undefiled before God, the Father, is this: to care for orphans and widows in their distress, and to keep oneself unstained by the world" (Jas 1:27). Indeed, faith need not be a deadly virtue but the life-giving grace of God, which touches us inside and out.

While walking the Camino de Santiago in Spain, I came to some startling conclusions about my own faith. Here I encountered many people, both religious and secular, from around the world. But every time I talked to people on the Way, I discovered that we always shared something in common. Perhaps it was a love of coffee, an experience, or a place. Sometimes these commonalities bridged into family similarities or parenting challenges. And some of us shared a common faith, a similar outlook about Jesus and his call to love.

Regardless, my faith was strengthened when I served another person on the Way or spoke to another's life situation or struggles. Others helped me. And I hope I helped them.

In these simple experiences on the Camino I find a profound truth: God always desires to do a new thing in us.

Sometimes new experiences are required for us to break out of our tried-and-tested ideas about faith. When our faith becomes comfortable, we need to be shaken, to experience God's grace anew. When we embrace the good news of Jesus Christ again, we discover a gospel ever fresh and pertinent to our time.

Two

FROM LOVING OUR WAY
TO GOD'S WAY OF LOVE

But I say to you, Love your enemies and pray for
those who persecute you, so that you may be children
of your Father in heaven; for he makes his sun rise
on the evil and on the good, and sends rain on the
righteous and on the unrighteous. For if you love
those who love you, what reward do you have? . . .
Be perfect, therefore, as your heavenly Father is perfect.

MATTHEW 5:44-46, 48

WE LIVE IN A LOVE-SATURATED SOCIETY. Or, rather, we are bombarded with music about the pleasures of love, movies that portray the triumph of love, advertising that promises love, greeting cards that express love, dating services designed to match lovers, and a myriad of images, themes, and voices that tell us "love is the answer." We might even say that love is what makes the world go round.

But love—as portrayed by cultural norms—is not necessarily love as Jesus expressed it. Rather, Jesus frequently pointed out the incongruities and deficiencies of the love we espouse, a love that can, if we are not careful, merely support our own prejudices or selfish outcomes. Our definitions of love are often self-serving, self-preserving, and shot through with more fear than faith. Love can even become a deadly virtue (as narrowly defined by our own susceptibilities and weaknesses).

As Jesus noted, it is easy to fall into an expression of love that merely supports our own needs and desires (Mt 5:43-47). But love, as expressed in gospel, is something else entirely.

> This is how God showed his love among us: He sent his one and only Son into the world that we might live through him. This is love: not that we loved God, but that he loved us and sent his Son as an atoning sacrifice for our sins. (1 Jn 4:9-10 NIV)

> God so loved the world that he gave his one and only Son, that whoever believes in him shall not perish but have eternal life. (Jn 3:16 NIV)

Love—when expressed with our own outcomes in mind—can become a deadly virtue. But love created in the crucible of God's mercy for the world sets us free.

Decades ago C. S. Lewis pointed out these incongruities in his book *The Four Loves*. Lewis, searching for romantic love and finding it rather late in life, came at the subject through the back door. Lewis began by pointing out the gospel's declaration that "God is love" (1 Jn 4:16) and then followed with a myriad of observations (biblical, social, and creedal) to demonstrate how difficult this love is and what it demands of us. As Lewis pointed out, our love is most often (and maybe even completely) saturated with our own need. Rarely are we devoid of some element of self-preservation, weakness, or need when we seek or give love. What we commonly call *love*, according to Lewis, is most often greedy and exacting, and we even set up our love as a god and worship it. But this love is not the love of the gospel and is most assuredly one-sided. As Lewis noted, we look *to give* love. But only God *is* love.

Lewis does offer some bright spots for our consideration, however. He notes that the gospel word for love—*agapē*—could most efficiently be expressed as "charity," if we could retain the older connotation of that word. Here, Lewis points out that *charity* once connoted self-emptying or self-denial, even sacrifice. But even *agapē* love can be mishandled and abused by our respective theologies, and what we commonly end up with is a God who loves *like* us rather than a God whose love is not dependent on us.

Near the end of *The Four Loves*, Lewis points out that God *is love* and we are not. However, even in our weak imaginings and our human need to give and receive love, we are giving witness to the love of God, for we were made by God out of love. Here is how Lewis expresses it:

> For the dream of finding our end, the thing we were made for, in a heaven of purely human love could not be true unless our whole Faith were wrong. We were made for God. Only by being in some respect like Him, only be being a manifestation of His beauty, loving-kindness, wisdom or goodness, has any earthly Beloved excited our love. It is not that we have loved them too much, but that we did not quite understand what we were loving.[1]

This is just one of love's dilemmas. Lewis digs deeper into the matter by pointing out that our loves (both giving and receiving) are driven by our human need, but holds out the promise of being swallowed up by God's incomprehensible love, even as we make our weak and failed attempts at it.

In short, Lewis teaches that the gospel is expressed when we know the One who first loved us. Once we have received this divine love, we can then give love as God intended. We are dependent on God's love to define our human expressions of love.

ONCE WE HAVE RECEIVED THIS DIVINE LOVE, WE CAN THEN GIVE LOVE AS GOD INTENDED.

But we don't have to read C. S. Lewis or delve deeply into theology to note the strange landscape of love humans have created. What passes for love is often weak and ineffectual, or at times trite and fleeting. Love, as we often encounter it, feeds us briefly or offers a glimmer of hope, but it frequently fades or grows dull. And in faith circles we often prop ourselves up under the prospect of acting in love, while at the same time being motivated by attitudes that reveal quite the opposite.

Consider, for example, our weakness in dealing with those different from ourselves. Our tendencies toward rejection are strong, even in those who espouse love. And we are often left in a muddle of sorting through our own fears and doubts before we can truly love the stranger, welcome the broken, or embrace those of a different faith, background, or culture.

Some years ago I came face to face with these tendencies in my own faith. (I still deal with them daily.) Our congregation, at the time, was one of the few in the city that offered prenatal and postnatal care to women in the form of clothing, car seats, toiletries, and baby food. Every week, whenever the pantry was open, women would arrive to pick up supplies for their infants. Most of these women were young, single moms. They often arrived at the pantry with noticeable embarrassment, anguish, or pain. Some, however, were bitter or angry, and I didn't do well in handling certain situations.

I always prayed before I worked the pantry, asking God to give me love and wisdom. But there were times when I felt justified in offering "tough love" to some women who were promiscuous, demanding, and flippant. I sometimes found myself giving lectures or withholding certain items from those with a bad attitude. And a few times I recall closing these difficult conversations by offering platitudes such as "God loves you" or "God bless you."

Afterwards, I knew I had failed to love as God loves. I wondered, *How should I love in these situations?* While it felt good to unload my advice on some of the frequent "customers," this good feeling didn't last long. I would go home feeling lousy, knowing that I had failed to love. I would make promises to God and to myself, hoping to do better next time. But in a few weeks I would repeat the same mistakes, lashing out "in love."

I discovered I could not always love as Jesus loved. It *is* difficult to love—and perhaps it is most difficult to love ourselves, which is why we are unkind to others.

I am reminded of a Jewish parable, the story of a famous rabbi who was a man of prayer. One day he prayed, "Lord of the Universe, give me the strength and wisdom to change the world." But after weeks of struggle and failure, the rabbi realized he could not change the world. And so he prayed, "Lord, give me the strength and wisdom to change my city." But again, after some time, the rabbi noticed that he was having little effect on his town. Again he approached God and prayed, "Lord, give me the strength and wisdom to change my congregation." Weeks elapsed, but again the rabbi noted that he was unable to change others. Again he prayed, "Lord, give me now the strength and wisdom to change those closest to me." But in due time the rabbi noticed that even his wife and children were difficult people, and he couldn't change them. At last he prayed, "Lord, I have been unable to change the world, my city, my congregation, or my family. But at least give me the wisdom and the strength to change myself."[2]

Such is our condition in love. As Jesus noted, we are in a precarious situation when it comes to this virtue. On the one hand we are asked to love as God loves. But we usually fail to love in the highest sense of the word. We offer love when it is convenient, draws attention to ourselves, or when others are watching. But at the end of the day we note our many failed attempts at love, attempts that call attention to our own brokenness and weaknesses.

Love is difficult.

Consider, for example, Christian people who affirm their love for humanity, but hate individuals. Or consider how many people love freedom, but turn love on its head by working against equal rights for others. We hear about those who purport to love God so much that they kill others in order to "save life" or "protect" the faithful. Idolatry comes in many forms, and often our idols show up in the form of our virtues—with love often being the prime culprit.

Jesus spoke to these misplaced virtues.

Luke's version of Christ's teachings has a more practical description of love. Here, Jesus not only asks his followers to love their enemies but urges active followthrough—even toward the ungrateful and the wicked. "Love your enemies, do good, and lend, expecting nothing in return. Your reward will be great; and you will be children of the Most High; for he is kind to the ungrateful and the wicked. Be merciful, just as your Father is merciful" (Lk 6:35-36).

Love described by Jesus is remarkable; it's an action rather than an emotion, an innate concern for those who might even hate or despise us. Only one living in the Spirit can accomplish such love. When we think of this incredible action and how it might play out in our own world, we are at once enlivened and defeated by its very nature. Perhaps this is what Jesus had in mind. Love may call us to ask the unanswerable question, *Is such a love possible?*

Love Goals

Leo Buscaglia, a professor of special education at the University of Southern California in the late 1960s, was grading essays in his office one day when he happened to receive word of a student's death. This student, who was enrolled in Buscaglia's class, had committed suicide soon after turning in the essay. Moved by this tragedy, Buscaglia began working on a syllabus for a new class he wanted to teach: Love 1A.

Many of Buscaglia's colleagues were skeptical. How could love be taught? Would students enroll in such a class? Why should a love class be offered for credit?

Undeterred by these concerns, Buscaglia pressed on and offered his Love 1A class as an elective. No one could not have predicted the results. The class was a hit with students, and in time it became the most popular class at USC. Love was not only the topic, but students who took Buscaglia's class sincerely wanted to study love in lieu of the popular love-ins and lovefests of the 1970s. Buscaglia's love class also helped him to generate many bestselling books on love. (His first, *Love*, remains a bestseller long after Buscaglia's death.)

Through his class Buscaglia came to realize that love was the ultimate goal of most people. People were not only looking for love but also wanted to give love. And yet love remained elusive, a high ideal few people believed they had achieved.

Buscaglia, however, pressed on into the study of love and love's ideal. Over the years he began to write and speak passionately about the possibilities of love, even extravagant and self-sacrificial love, and its potential in human existence. Buscaglia was offering modern-day examples of love lived, not just as an academic discipline, but as he had learned it from his Catholic faith. The love he was sharing in essays and books was epitomized by Jesus, who was love embodied. Buscaglia came to believe that love could be a goal, even if not fully attained. More than a theory, love was only love when it was lived in actuality. In short, only love in action was love.

When "love" is self-serving and possessive (even pagans love those who love them back, Jesus says), it becomes a deadly virtue. But according to Jesus, sacrificial and grace-filled love is life giving. Love of this nature is not mere morality but a way of life that determines our and our neighbors' future. Love is not an emotion but a way fraught with great difficulty, devotion, and decision.

> WHEN "LOVE" IS SELF-SERVING AND POSSESSIVE, IT BECOMES A DEADLY VIRTUE.

M. Scott Peck's classic book *The Road Less Traveled* begins with a three-word sentence: "Life is difficult." And so it is. This terse phrase well describes the path of love as well. Love is difficult, according to Jesus. Trading love for hate is difficult. Loving through life's tragedies and hardships and violence is all the more remarkable. This love—God's love that first loved us—is gospel.

But can it be understood and lived?

Decades ago one school of thought (most notably led by Albert Schweitzer in his *Quest of the Historical Jesus*) contended that Jesus gave his disciples an "interim ethic"—a way of life that could be lived in the short term but was not achievable in the long pull of human experience. This school of thought believed that such teaching on love could not be practiced over a lifetime.

However, this perspective guts Jesus' teachings of their power. Instead, we see that Christ's requirements press the boundaries of our deepest loves and call forth love as a transformative action.

Love is a verb and not a noun. Jesus both calls us *into his love* and to *love others as he loved*. St. Paul makes this distinction between being "in Christ" and having "Christ in us." The latter is a phrase Paul rarely if ever uses—though it has been popularized by many who espouse "personal" salvation and by the prominent forms of individualistic Christianity today. Paul would, I think, say that we love when we are "in Christ," when we know that God first loved us.

Faith is being "in Christ," and we learn how to love more deeply when we first understand that we are loved by God.

These are the distinctions Jesus is making about the nature of love. *Agapē* (love) is not a personal commodity; we do not claim it as our own. *Agapē* is not merely loving those who are kind, agreeable, or receptive to the love we offer. Love is no respecter of persons. As Jesus points out, our goal is to love those who may have no regard for us at all, no understanding, even, that they have received love or even care a whit about it. Love, as the highest ideal and goal of the Christian, is to love as God loves—without regard, without expectation of reward, without delineation or withholding.

There is a tendency in our popular theologies to say we love others while qualifying it (and quantifying it?) by our personal judgments or strong feelings about sin. Jesus asks his followers to love others, especially enemies and those who will never repay in kindness or mercy. Jesus never used the phrase *love the sinner, but hate the sin.* He simply asked his followers to love, especially those who would not repay in love.

Love, as Jesus describes it, is action that crosses boundaries. In many of Jesus' teachings love is embodied as care that breaks through political or social mores (for example, the parable of the good Samaritan) or as concern for those ostracized from the religious community. Love also crosses economic, racial, and ethnic barriers and seeks the best for others.

In today's criticisms of the church, many do not understand why the church isn't more loving. They see the church as more judgmental than loving, more critical than caring. This is a great challenge to the Christian community. We walk a fine line between teaching truth in love or embodying truth in caring action.

A few months ago I had a conversation with a young man who expressed his disengagement with the church as follows:

> The church seems hypocritical to my generation. The church seems preoccupied with sex or at least wants to judge and control the erotic love of others. But on the other hand the church seems unwilling to demonstrate what love truly is. Isn't love showing concern for the poor and the outcast? I don't understand why the church gives so much attention and lip service to judging other people's love while ignoring the deepest needs in the world. Why not show what love is instead of condemning it?

While I felt judged by this young man's perception (and also misunderstood), I also heard what he was saying. Often those who are critical of the church long for exemplary love. And perhaps this is where we fall down most—in our inability to exhibit love before we teach truth.

My takeaway from the conversation was that the church needs to embody and demonstrate love. But we could also do a better job of communicating the historical faith. Though not entirely accurate, this young man's complaint about the church's preoccupation with erotic love versus *agapē* love had some traction. But I invited him to look for expressions of Christian love where the weak and the needy *are* cared for, where Christ *is* evident in acts of service. I invited him to look more deeply at the church. I also prayed that God would give me a more extravagant love.

Such is our human predicament and our spiritual brokenness. To love as God loves seems like an impossibility, but at the same time Christ calls us to be perfect as our heavenly Father is perfect (Mt 5:48).

These ideas are clearly evident in church history. John Wesley taught much about love, which he regarded as the highest goal or ideal of the Christian life. Wesley believed that when Jesus spoke of being perfect, love was his ideal. But Wesley also offered some practical rules for those who were seeking to attain a holy life.

In Wesley's three simple rules he admonished his societies to "First—do no harm. Second—do good. And third—stay in love with God."[3] Wesley insisted that the teachings of Christ are attainable. Christ asked his disciples to be perfect (or "complete"). And he also asked his disciples to love perfectly, as the heavenly Father loves.

Wesley certainly did not believe that a Christian could be perfect in all things. Far from it. He insisted that Christians are sinners saved by grace. But he believed it was possible to be perfected in love, to see the world and others through the eyes of the Father, who loves the whole world. In fact, Methodist pastors, as part of their ordination vows, are still asked two questions about love:

- Are you going on to perfection?

- Do you expect to be made perfect in love in this life?

In many contemporary theologies we can see how the love of God has been turned into something monstrous (even by well-meaning people). A recent church billboard, for example, touting John 3:16 also displayed scenes reminiscent of a hellish inferno, as if Jesus' teaching "for God so loved the world" was a threat—especially a threat to those poor, unfortunate souls who didn't belong to the congregation who rented the billboard.

Likewise, it's not uncommon today to hear church people talk about "tough love," which rejects certain behaviors and people as a means of showing *real* love. Many of these tough-love strategies, however, are nothing but *tough*, and don't reveal the love Jesus practiced with his life, suffering, and death. Such love may be tough, indeed, but it is not redemptive or self-sacrificial. The toughest love, according to Jesus, extends our hearts, hands, and hope to those who are broken, bruised, and bewildered. This love is made all the more difficult because many will not receive it. Love is tough because it requires the best use of our minds and our wills. Jesus sends forth the church to embody this holy and tough love—serving, sacrificing, and calling others into the love of Jesus himself.

Love Is . . .

Søren Kierkegaard was a theologian, philosopher, and a teller of tales. His parables often illustrated some spiritual dilemma or offered answers to deeper questions about life, God, and love. In one such parable Kierkegaard offers the story of two painters. The first said, "I have travelled the world, but have been unable to find a man worthy of painting. Whenever I see a face, I note only the flaws and deficiencies. Therefore I seek in vain."

The second painter said, "I have not travelled the world. My work has kept me close to home. But when I look at the faces of those closest to me, I see that each one's flaws and deficiencies mask at least one redeeming quality. Therefore I paint, and am satisfied."[4]

This beautiful parable illustrates, among other things, the nature of love. Love is an action compelling us to see the best in others, and by doing so changes relationships. Love that views others through a lens of criticism (moral love) is not the same as love that embraces the redeeming qualities of God's mercy (agapē love). Agapē loves in spite of apparent flaws. But our human tendencies and definitions commonly embrace the former and not the latter.

But this is an old dilemma.

We often consider the early church as unified in theology and practice. But in fact the early church was quite diverse. There were various schools of thought (Jerusalem, Antioch, and Alexandria) and alternative communities (the desert fathers of Syria and in Northern Africa). The alternative communities especially gave rise to renewed expressions of agapē love. And many parables on love have survived from this era.

One such parable goes like this: A disciple approached the abbot and said, "Tell me, Father, what would you do if you saw a brother sleeping during worship? Would you pinch him and reprimand him?" The abbot responded, "On the contrary, if I saw a brother sleeping during the worship, I would assume he is tired. I would make my lap his pillow and let him sleep."[5]

Agapē love. Mercy. Love sacrificial.

Jesus, of course, made love his trump card. In typical rabbinic fashion he once answered the question, "What is the greatest commandment in the Torah?" in similar spirit to that of his predecessor, the rabbi Hillel: "The greatest commandment is: love the Lord your God with all your heart, soul, mind and strength, and love your neighbor as yourself" (see Mt 22:37; Mk 12:30; Lk 10:27). This question also provides a glimpse into the varied expressions of the early church. Many centered on ideas like, What is the core of the Christian faith? What is the gospel? What is the greatest of Jesus' teachings or commandments? How do we understand them in our time?

The Gospels were written with various audiences in mind (Greek, Roman, Jewish). One early tradition—the Johannine— can be seen in the interplay between the Gospel and the Epistles of John. At the center is a most challenging extrapolation of love. For example, note how the following biblical passages from the Johannine tradition—building on Christ's new commandment—define *agapē* love in an ever-broadening (and challenging) manner.

> For God so loved the world that he gave his only Son, so that everyone who believes in him may not perish but may have eternal life. Indeed, God did not send the Son into the world to condemn the world, but in order that the world might be saved through him. (Jn 3:16-17)

> God's love was revealed among us in this way: God sent his only Son into the world so that we might live through him. In this is love, not that we loved God but that he loved us and sent his Son to be the atoning sacrifice for our sins. Beloved, since God loved us so much, we also ought to love one another. (1 Jn 4:9-11)

I give you a new commandment, that you love one another. Just as I have loved you, you also should love one another. By this everyone will know that you are my disciples, if you have love for one another. (Jn 13:34-35)

And this is love, that we walk according to his commandments; this is the commandment just as you heard it from the beginning—you must walk in it. (2 Jn 6)

Beloved, let us love one another, because love is from God; everyone who loves is born of God and knows God. Whoever does not love does not know God, for God is love. (1 Jn 4:7-8)

These were the challenges of *agapē* love in this ancient tradition, and as a definition of love they compel us to broaden our own understandings and actions. This tradition even speaks to the deadly virtue of love (narrowly defined and broadly understood). But it also offers a compelling journey into love that is perfected by our actions and faith in God's sacrificial and redemptive love.

Perhaps we can see how love is manifest through even small acts and seemingly insignificant moments of care. Mother Teresa gave voice to this. As part of a long series of theological questions, a reporter asked, "So, what do you believe about these [difficult or controversial] issues?" Mother Teresa responded, "I believe there's no such thing as luck in life; it's God's love."

> LOVE IS THE GOSPEL LIVED OUT.

And on another occasion, when challenged by the notion that we could change the world, Mother Teresa answered, "Not all of us can do great things. But we can do small things with great love."[6]

We gauge our theology of love based on our view of God. This was the inherent presupposition of the Johannine tradition, which insists that God's character (God *is* love) is embodied in and through our own love, most notably through our concern for those we may not ordinarily want to serve.

In order to avoid the deadly virtue of love we need to take our cues from Jesus and from the early Christian communities who defined love in action. Love is many things, perhaps, but no greater definitions exist than those we find in the Johannine tradition. This love is at once a great comfort and an enormous challenge. And Jesus is the example. Love is the gospel lived out.

Inside Out

One way to understand the nature of love is to work from the inside out. Jesus stressed this insight on many occasions, and it is one of the defining elements of classic evangelicalism: the notion that God can work change in the human heart. Jesus noted that we need this inner change—love that begins from the inside out—most of all.

This is no more apparent than in our limited definitions of love and the frequent ways we dole love out to those who are deserving of receiving it. Perhaps that is why there is so much anger in the world today. We have forgotten how to love. Many people only know how to hate.

A workshop for pastors I attended had the theme "Countering the Entitlement Culture in Church." The workshop explored the many ways entitlement attitude and culture has crept into the church. Many Christians now have a consumer mindset (rather than a servant mindset). Questions like, How will the church serve my needs? Who will help my family? or, What's in it for me? are far more prevalent than, Where can I serve? How can I help? or, What can I contribute to God's work? At its core the entitlement mindset places love of self above all other loves.

In short, the workshop reminded me that some forms of entitlement are at play in all our lives. (It's not a generational phenomenon.) As Jesus taught, some part of us desires to be loved far more than we desire to exhibit love. We are in a quandary. And when we don't receive what we think we deserve, we get angry.

There are many angry people in the world today. Some people wake up angry and go to bed angry. Many work side by side with people who, day in and day out, are filled with rage. Others are angry in their marriages, in their parenting, or simply at "them"— a faceless or nameless group of people they believe are responsible for the world's ills.

Jesus spoke about these realities too. He often paired our anger with our inability or unwillingness to love. Overcoming anger— and expressing love in its wake—go hand in hand. Jesus taught that we overcome anger with love, which is movement, action, and reconciliation.

> But I say to you that if you are angry with a brother or sister, you will be liable to judgment; and if you insult a brother or sister, you will be liable to the council; and if you say, "You fool," you will be liable to the hell of fire. So when you are offering your gift at the altar, if you remember that your sister or brother has something against you, leave your gift there before the altar and go; first be reconciled to your brother or sister, and then come and offer your gift. (Mt 5:22-24)

> Why do you see the speck in your neighbor's eye, but do not notice the log in your own eye? Or how can you say to your neighbor, "Let me take the speck out of your eye," while the log is in your own eye? You hypocrite, first take the log out of your own eye, and then you will see clearly to take the speck out of your neighbor's eye. (Mt 7:3-5)

The greatest hindrance to love is anger unexpressed or anger expressed in unrestrained and violent words, behaviors, or outcomes. Our world is littered with this anger. And in the wake of these tendencies, love seems like a weak response. Love even seems foolish or like martyrdom.

Perhaps we fail to see that love is a greater force. And if the gospel is love—expressed in the cross and resurrection—our tendencies toward anger reveal our weaker selves. Jesus taught that love has already overtaken and overcome the world. St. Paul wrote that nothing can separate us from the love of God in Christ (Rom 8:38-39). However, even as followers of Jesus we sometimes forget this. We are most tempted to forget this truth during our darkest moments and most overwhelming crises in life.

In more recent years my wife and I have dealt with these truths about love in our own family. During my son's high school years he fell into depression, which often manifested itself in his seclusion, lack of focus in school, and anger often directed at us. We were at a loss. We sought the help of counselors, placed our son in alternative education, and put him through a battery of tests. But these steps seemed counterproductive and further enhanced the rift that was growing between us.

And we became angry. At every turn, with every new opportunity or offer, we were rebuffed or met with the incredible force of our son's rage. Although I was a pastor and had helped hundreds of people through similar situations, I felt stymied by my own son and began to feel guilty and bitter about the anger I, at times, felt toward him. My wife, though a teacher and principal, was also at a loss. And at times her anger toward my son seemed more than I could bear.

We were floundering. The three of us were often despondent. In tears. Broken.

But my wife and I also had conversations with other people who came alongside us with helpful insights and advice: "Don't stop loving. Be patient. Love even when it hurts. Love even when you do not receive love in return. Love through the fits and the fists and the fights. Don't retaliate. Just love. And when you have small openings to have meaningful conversation, make the best of them."

How telling. How truthful. And how life changing. As I write this today we are still growing into this remarkable love. All of us.

I have learned that anger and love are both transformative experiences. Anger is one path that we can choose, and it produces certain outcomes. Jesus was angry at times, and his anger produced responses. Outcomes.

Love is transformative also. This is the transformation Christ calls us to embrace. Love is often sacrificial. Sometimes love has to relax in the greater love of God. And though love is difficult, it is our highest aspiration and our highest calling in faith. It is not always easy to love—even those in our own households—but Christ asks us to love without regard, without pretense, without expectation. Love requires us to forgive, to seek reconciliation, told hold out hope. Love is powerful.

As Jesus pointed out, when we love only those who love us in return, our love becomes a deadly virtue. This love is useful only to ourselves, to fulfill our own ends. But when we love unconditionally, when we love those who are seemingly unlovable or unloving, something happens to us too. We become bigger people, more Christlike, more amazing.

Perhaps, like me, you are still growing toward this love. Like me, you have not yet arrived. But love is possible. For God *is love*. And it is most important that we try to love, that we attempt each day to embody some expression of Christ's love for the world. We can do this in our homes, in our classrooms, in our congregations. We are called to love outside the boundaries. Without this movement we lapse into self-absorption (even loving our own misery at times) and fail to reach out to those who might need God's love most of all.

Even famous theologians and experienced clergy have discovered love in unassuming ways.

Henri Nouwen, a well-known Catholic professor, priest, and writer, spent nine months toward the latter years of his life working at the L'Arche community in France—a network seeking to build community and home for those with intellectual disabilities. Although Nouwen had taught at top divinity schools, received academic acclaim, and wrote many bestselling books, he learned much about the nature of love from the gentle people of the L'Arche community.

These people, disabilities and all, received Father Nouwen unconditionally into their community. They taught him about love, but more importantly they demonstrated the *agapē* love Henri Nouwen had written about for most of his life. What he had learned and taught in the university he was now receiving without fanfare or acclaim. He was learning how to give love as well as receive it.

And that's an important lesson for all of us. We need to learn how to love ourselves if we are to love others. This is also part of love's power.

There are many who have not or cannot love themselves. Perhaps they have made mistakes, messed up, failed, or sinned too grievously, and these consequences have overwhelmed them. Their anger may come out in bitterness toward others. But Jesus asks us to love our neighbors as we love ourselves. And so we begin from the inside out to heal ourselves and offer love to others. In essence, Christians embody the love of Christ through the power of the Holy Spirit, who leads us into truth, which is the love God has for the world.

Love is the gospel, which is God's love for the world through Jesus Christ. This is the love we seek to express in word and deed.

One of my best friends often reminisces about a small sign that used to hang on his refrigerator as a child. His mother would recite this bit of wisdom, and it became a kind of mantra in their home: "The love in your heart is not meant to stay. It is not love until you give it away."

Myopic or self-preserving love is not love as taught by Jesus. It is not the love taught by St. Paul (1 Cor 13). God *is love*.

We give love away because God loved first.

Three

FROM FOCUSING ON OUR FAMILY TO SEEING GOD'S FAMILY FIRST

When we cry, "Abba! Father!" it is that very
Spirit bearing witness with our spirit that we
are children of God, and if children, then heirs,
heirs of God and joint heirs with Christ.

ROMANS 8:15-17

THE MOVIE *THE RON CLARK STORY* offers a beautiful portrait of the power of family, though not in the traditional sense. Based on a true-life story, high school teacher Ron Clark journeys from the safety and security of his hometown to Harlem, where, not surprisingly, he encounters a classroom of students who have been identified as "unteachable" and "incorrigible." Most of the students in Ron's class are from low-income families. Some have criminal records; others, violent tendencies. All have given up on themselves and their futures. None of them hold out any hope for or promise of a better life.

Over a course of weeks, however, Clark earns the trust and respect of his students. Although it is an arduous teaching endeavor fraught with anger, tears, and setbacks, the students eventually see themselves through their teacher's eyes. Utilizing firm discipline, practical rules, and a fair amount of creative teaching techniques, Ron gradually changes the attitudes and outlooks of his students.

But the learning does not begin—and the students do not change—until they see their own value. There is no transformation until Ron's first rule becomes the mantra of every student: *We are a family.*

While watching *The Ron Clark Story* it becomes apparent that family is paramount in our human relationships and our yearning for love, acceptance, and value. But family is much broader and more inclusive than our flesh-and-blood relations. In fact, the biblical concept of family—which is central to the gospel understanding of the church—calls us to demonstrate radical hospitality to those who are not part of our clan. Our welcome extends to the outcast and the marginalized. Our love and relationships are birthed in care for others, even those who may be difficult to love (just like those in our flesh-and-blood families).

Today, people yearn for family that will not break apart or succumb to narcissism, divorce, dissatisfaction, or individualism. These patterns are especially ingrained in the contemporary Western mindset. While family seems to be highly valued in the church, it's difficult to keep family together, to build long-lasting and meaningful relationships. In short, for all of our talk about how important family is, it's difficult to perceive this importance based on the outcomes.

WE NEED TO BROADEN OUR CONCEPT TO INCLUDE FAMILY AS JESUS OFFERED IT.

Perhaps our idea of the Christian family has been misplaced. Our concept of family may be too small, too narrow, when compared to the family of God that Jesus offers. We may benefit from exchanging our flesh-and-blood views of family for one built on faith, love, and the Spirit. Family togetherness is a virtue, but we need to broaden our concept to include family as Jesus offered it.

When Jesus returned to his hometown, word of his arrival spread. People gathered to hear him teach. His family showed up, wanting to have time alone with him.

> They said to him, "Your mother and your brothers and sisters are outside, asking for you." And he replied, "Who are my mother and my brothers?" And looking at those who sat around him, he said, "Here are my mother and my brothers! Whoever does the will of God is my brother and sister and mother." (Mk 3:32-35)

Mark doesn't tell us how Mary and the rest of the family responded to this new family concept. Were they hurt? Troubled? Bothered? Angered? We don't know. But we gain a broader concept of family. Jesus seems to be saying, "I've got a much larger family than those standing outside the door. I'm including others. Anyone who does the will of God is family."

This is a radical concept, one that the church has attempted to embrace throughout the centuries. The church is not a compilation of individual families, but one remarkable family of God where many are embraced, welcomed, and valued.

Jesus spoke often of this family of God and gave his life to make us brothers and sisters. In fact, he challenges our small concept of family, stating that our vision and embrace of the kingdom of God is tempered by our ability (or inability) to leave behind our blood relationships for the greater gift of the church. These teachings are challenging, to be sure.

Consider, in this light, what Jesus taught about the family of God and our proclivity to become self-centered and self-absorbed within our respective families:

Whoever loves father or mother more than me is not worthy of me; and whoever loves son or daughter more than me is not worthy of me; and whoever does not take up the cross and follow me is not worthy of me. (Mt 10:37-38)

Everyone who has left houses or brothers or sisters or father or mother or children or fields, for my name's sake, will receive a hundredfold, and will inherit eternal life. (Mt 19:29)

Another of his disciples said to him, "Lord, first let me go and bury my father." But Jesus said to him, "Follow me, and let the dead bury their own dead." (Mt 8:21-22)

Jesus sets high priority on his family, which is missional in tone. We need this family in order to follow Jesus into ministry. Yes, our individual families can do these things, but Jesus reveals that, in the light of eternity, our individual families are part of the larger family of God. We are all one in the kingdom of God.

God's Big Family

Throughout the Gospels, Jesus speaks of God as his Father (*Abba*, or Daddy, in Aramaic). From this we learn about the care of our God. Jesus makes it clear that the God of Abraham, Isaac, and Jacob is not just our Creator—invisible, immutable, incomprehensible—but also the Father who has come near to his children, who is not far off but hears our prayers and comes to our aid. These ideas about God are important as we consider our call to be the family of God. Instead of thinking small, we see the big family Jesus had in mind.

Some years ago I led a weekend retreat for the men of the church. We had come together to discuss how we could be better fathers, husbands, and servants. There was ample time for worship, study, and individual reflection. Naturally, not all of the men were married. Some were divorced. Others had never married. We were younger and older. Some had been active in the church for decades, others for just a few months. Some had a mature faith; others were new to the faith. Nevertheless, everyone had insights that benefitted the retreat.

One of the most memorable conversations that weekend came while we were discussing the family. One man, who had been married for decades and who had three grown children, said, "I have had many memorable experiences as a husband and father. My family means the world to me. But I have noted through the years that my most valuable spiritual experiences—those places and times when I have felt very close to God and to others—have not occurred at home or with my family. In fact, the most profound Christian experiences I have had always occur when I have stretched myself beyond the comforts of my family. Perhaps this is what Jesus meant by warning us to look beyond our individual families to see the larger picture of what God is unfolding in other relationships, especially those who do not yet know the love of God."

For the next hour we all noted how easy it is to become absorbed in our own families, to lose sight of what marriage, parenting, and home are all about: giving witness to the kingdom of God. On that weekend retreat we talked about our society's strong pull toward sports, entertainment, and financial security. We were all struggling to come to terms with Jesus' command to seek first the kingdom of God (Mt 6:33). We all wanted to be good husbands, fathers, and providers, but we had also glimpsed the big family Jesus has in mind for us, something much larger than ourselves and our own pursuits.

As we think about the misplaced virtue of family, we should also note the number of people who yearn to be a part of a family. These insights are important. Perhaps this lost family (or a desire for lasting relationships) may be what younger people are looking for in gangs or in drugs, alcohol, violence, or promiscuity. Many of these "families" promise to provide security, belonging, and a cause. As misplaced as these are, we can see how shared hatreds and common goals can be an allure to people on the edge of loneliness, despair, or poverty. At its root, we long for loving relationships and purpose for our lives. We long for God's family in one way or another. St. Augustine put it well: "Our hearts are restless till they find rest in Thee."[1]

Thankfully, we have the gospel. Those looking for a cause, for acceptance, for belonging and welcome can find it in the gracious embrace of the church. This is what Jesus taught and millions have experienced. Our small, individual families are but a faint shadow of the big family of God, and we aim to make the kingdom of God known in loving actions of word and deed, and to invite others into God's household.

> OUR SMALL, INDIVIDUAL FAMILIES ARE BUT A FAINT SHADOW OF THE BIG FAMILY OF GOD.

I have had many discussions with pastors of inner-city churches in the heartland who are trying desperately to overcome the influence of gangs. Many children and teenagers, especially boys, are being swept up into the hollow promises of belonging and connection. They believe their futures are defined by these relationships and the honors afforded through criminal activities.

In suburbia, the allure of family activities is equally strong. Many Christian families are distracted from the call of Christ by a full lineup of activities—sports, leisure, vacations—designed to keep family together but often having the opposite effect. Many Christian families spend little time or money on God's work, but are fully invested in their children's work.

I have encountered these forms of idolatry in my own family, but there is hope, especially when we glimpse the family of God in action.

Not long ago I had a conversation with a grandfather who came to my office asking if his grandson could confirm his faith in Jesus and be baptized. The grandfather recounted how the parents had abandoned their son, how he had become his grandson's legal guardian. I was moved. I began meeting with this thirteen-year-old boy, and I was impressed by his knowledge of Jesus, his sincerity, and his deep desire to be a part of the household of faith.

Our conversations and study were holy moments for me. And our church celebrated his baptism. Congregational members wrote keepsake letters. Others stepped forward as godparents. Still others provided special music and testimony. Many later commented that they had glimpsed heaven and finally understood what the family of God was about. The family of God is the hope for the nuclear family.

Churches hold out the family of God as an alternative to the idolatry of the family. Some congregations are "adopting" troubled or at-risk teens, helping them out of harm's way and into a new life. Others are walking for peace in the streets or organizing job fairs that connect young people with mentors and friends, a larger family who cares. People who know no family are finding God's family. This is the church in action; it's the family Jesus had in mind.

Not long ago I received a phone call from an old friend who informed me of a tragedy in his life. We had grown up together, and for as long as I had known him, he was in poor health. Most of his childhood and adolescence had been spent in hospital rooms. And now he was calling to tell me that his wife had died following a long struggle with brain cancer. *Wow*, I thought, *and now another struggle!*

But as we talked on the phone I detected hope in my friend's voice. I asked, "What has made the difference?" "I couldn't have made it without my church family," he answered. "So many people have come alongside me, helped in profound and practical ways. Some even helped with the funeral expenses."

Church family. Big family. Connections and relationships far more meaningful than our flesh-and-blood ties. That's what Jesus was speaking to.

The family of God, according to Jesus, takes precedence over our individual family commitments. In fact, our individual families may sometimes be the source of our deepest frustrations and disappointments. Of course, we also experience deep joy and love in our individual families, but we dare not become myopic or narrow, thinking that our family joys or sorrows define our experience with God. There is always more. And when our families embrace others with the same care and love we enjoy in our homes, this becomes a testimony to the family of God.

Whenever we consider the virtues of family, we would do well to keep the big picture in mind—for God's family is indeed very large. We are no less a part of Abraham's family (or Martha's or Paul's) than we are our individual heritages. Our ties run deep, and the picture Jesus offers is one of lasting significance, deep meaning, and eternal belonging. In one way or another, we are all searching for these ties.

In fact, there is more to the big family than I can name here.

Family Ties

The apostle Paul also picked up on the theme of the family of God. In his Corinthian correspondence Paul admonishes that congregation for their self-centeredness and selfishness, for looking after their clans and individual interests. He attempts to teach them the greatest way, the way of love (1 Cor 13), which once again points to the church as a family of God.

In his letter to the churches of Galatia, Paul points out that God is calling the church to be more than a collection of tribes but the living body of Christ, the true family of God. Note how often Paul refers to the church as "sisters and brothers" and how his theology leads the church to embrace the idea of being one family in Jesus.

> There is no longer Jew or Greek, there is no longer slave or free, there is no longer male and female; for all of you are one in Christ Jesus. (Gal 3:28)

> When the fullness of time had come, God sent his Son, born of a woman, born under the law, in order to redeem those who were under the law, so that we might receive adoption as children. (Gal 4:4-5)

> Whenever we have an opportunity, let us work for the good of all, and especially for those of the family of faith. (Gal 6:10)

Paul is writing to a Gentile audience—various tribes and clans who do not see themselves as having connection with the Jewish faith, but who desire to be a part of the new Israel, the family of God. Essentially, Paul is telling these disconnected peoples, with their respective cultures and traditions, that they are now part of the household of God, a gift they have received by the grace of God through faith.

These ancient words hold promise and hope for us too. God is still doing a new thing, forming new connections, new understandings, new families that can be welcomed into the larger family of God. Paul offers this grand theology to the churches. And when we hear it, it may seem contemporary to us.

It is amazing to note how often we in the West find ourselves longing for a deeper appreciation for the family. Our popular music speaks to this theme. And many movies and television programs over the past thirty years portray both the brokenness of family and the longing we have to discover true identity and love.

Despite the various tribes and traditions our Christian brothers and sisters come from, we all bring something to the body of Christ, the household of faith. We need each other in order to be whole, to be complete in our understanding and faith.

> GOD IS STILL DOING A NEW THING, FORMING NEW CONNECTIONS, NEW UNDERSTANDINGS, NEW FAMILIES THAT CAN BE WELCOMED INTO THE LARGER FAMILY OF GOD.

One of the favorite books on my shelves is Richard Foster's *Streams of Living Water: Celebrating the Great Traditions of Christian Faith*. In this book Foster identifies six major traditions in the church: contemplative, holiness, charismatic, social justice, evangelical, and incarnational. Foster's exceptional work traces each of these traditions through Christian history, celebrating the ways these expressions of faith have touched us through the formation of monastic and prayer traditions, through liturgical developments, through reformations, movements, and through the paradigm shifts that transformed the church and touched the world.

Some years ago I was blessed to share this book with other pastors serving in traditions other than my own. As we studied this book, I was amazed by how our respective traditions and tribes each brought something of importance, clarity, or understanding to the Christian faith. It was moving to see how each of us learned to appreciate the insights of the others' traditions.

Comments ranged from "I've gained a new appreciation for the saints" to "I've never thought of spiritual gifts in this light" to "I'm very grateful for the liturgy that has been preserved for centuries." In essence, we not only learned how to appreciate each other but also became brothers and sisters in Christ. Differences did not necessarily vanish, but we learned that our spiritual bonds, our faith in Christ, bound us together in the family of God.

These ideas are, of course, inherent in the Bible.

For example, in his epistles Paul is giving us a new vision of family. He's demonstrating that God is doing a new thing, a bigger thing. God is forming a new society rooted in love, where people care for one another and regard each other as spiritual sisters and brothers. He holds out the hope that Jews and Gentiles, slaves and free, males and females can build on the foundation of our new relationship with Jesus and become the family of God. He asks Jesus' followers to see themselves as intricately linked together in a new body (1 Cor 12) in which people love and care for one another in practice and not just theory (1 Cor 13). At our best the church certainly does these things. God's family is revealed when we live up to the highest aspirations of hospitality, acceptance, and unconditional love. This happens when we regard others as our sisters and brothers.

A few years ago I was traveling through a rural area and had lost my way. By God's providence I drove by a small church with several cars in the adjacent lot. I parked, walked into the church to ask for directions, and was surprised to find myself front and center in some type of community food pantry.

What amazed me about this small congregation was the impact this handful of people was having in their community. These people obviously had discovered their mission, and the people who had gathered in the church to receive a small box of food had no intention of leaving quickly. Church and community were one; the folks who had come to receive the food wanted to hang out with those who were providing it. The food pantry was a community meeting place; friends sat with friends for conversation and a cup of coffee. The church wasn't providing a handout to strangers but a hand up to neighbors they knew by name, people who were loved and accepted as part of the family of God.

I did ask for directions that day, but I stayed long enough to experience the warmth of the people and to celebrate a little country church with a huge heart. If I had lived nearby, I would have been honored to attend the church or even serve as their pastor. This was truly the family of God, and I could sense that greater things than a box of food were being exchanged. People with varying gifts were willing to help each other. They exhibited a caring spirit that made them the family of God. I knew others would want to be a part of that community.

I wonder if Paul didn't have some of these family ties in mind when he wrote about breaking down barriers, no longer acknowledging our differences, or at least not acknowledging the old ways that have bound humanity in racism, sexism, ageism, and myriad other forms of brokenness that continue to enslave us in fear, misunderstanding, and violence. Instead, Paul hoped that in seeing the image of God in each other and recognizing the varied gifts that exist among us, we would discover the family of God.

God's New Creation

I know many couples who have adopted children. These couples have provided a home (and hope) to children who might otherwise have been relegated to orphanages, foster care, or life on the street. These adoptions have proven that parenting (and all that goes with it) is a powerful gift. Unconditional love, acceptance, nurture, security, and more demonstrate that *mother* and *father* aren't defined by our abilities to *procreate* but by our ability to *create* family. This affirmation was one of the earliest gifts of the church, especially in a first-century world where children were aborted, abandoned, or considered property. Time and again Scripture indicates that the early church was concerned with all of God's creation, especially the least of these. Jesus even equated the kingdom of God with becoming like a child in our wonder and awe of God's goodness.

The Scriptures speak of God's goodness and our adoption as children of God: "See what great love the Father has lavished on us, that we should be called children of God! And that is what we are!" (1 Jn 3:1 NIV). The family of God is an important theme in Scripture. We catch a glimpse of this in the way Jesus welcomed children.

People were bringing even infants to him that he might touch them; and when the disciples saw it, they sternly ordered them not to do it. But Jesus called for them and said, "Let the little children come to me, and do not stop them; for it is to such as these that the kingdom of God belongs. Truly I tell you, whoever does not receive the kingdom of God as a little child will never enter it." (Lk 18:15-17)

This is fascinating on many levels. First, it overturns our sensibilities and the high value we place on maturity and adulthood.

We typically equate faith with understanding or learning. Second, it reminds us that often we are like those "mature" disciples who see God's work as reserved for older people. Finally, the teaching creates a stir because Jesus welcomes the many—even those who lack deeper understanding—into the family. We like to hold to our respective places, often places of power, prestige, name recognition, or honor. But when we think about family, we know that children come first. Being the family of God invites us to turn our values upside down ("the first shall be last") and give honor and privilege to others regardless of age, income, intellect, or station. Being the church is truly a family affair of the highest calling, one that both threatens us and enlivens us to the very presence of God.

Sometimes those young fishers and tax collectors understood this new family dynamic, but other times it was lost on them. But we see glimpses of understanding.

> Peter said, "Look, we have left our homes and followed you." And he said to them, "Truly I tell you, there is no one who has left house or wife or brothers or parents or children, for the sake of the kingdom of God, who will not get back very much more in this age, and in the age to come eternal life." (Lk 18:28-30)

Indeed, we do gain "much more" in this age when we accept others as our sisters and brothers. I have known many across the years who have lost family members to death, distance, rejection, or misunderstandings. But many of these have gained new family. Some people have come alongside those in grief or welcomed the abandoned into their homes. Others have cared for broken families and, in very tangible ways, have been more loving than their blood relatives. The widow, the orphan, the oppressed—all are welcome in God's household. This is what Jesus had in mind.

Some years ago, our extended family gathered for a Sunday afternoon picnic at a city park. Over a hundred people—distant cousins, uncles and aunts, in-laws—came together to get introduced, reacquainted, and well fed. After we had blessed the food and gone through the food lines, someone noticed an older man sitting by himself in one corner of the shelter. He seemed content, enjoying his heaping plate of food and his iced tea. Someone asked, "Did he come *with you*? Is he *your* cousin?" Others assumed the man was a distant uncle or had married into the family.

Eventually word got around that this fellow simply wandered into our family reunion and helped himself to the food. But no one minded. There was more than enough to go around. And when it came time to play the annual softball game in the park, this stranger was invited to join us—and he did! What a blessing. For that day, at least, this stranger became part of our family, and we got to know him and his situation. We came together, fed him, gave him money to fix his motorcycle, and helped him return to his clan in another part of the state. And for at least that day I like to think we were the church, welcoming the stranger, calling a friend our brother.

Perhaps the first-century church in Jerusalem expressed this type of family. At least it appears so from what we read in the book of Acts. "All who believed were together and had all things in common; they would sell their possessions and goods and distribute the proceeds to all, as any had need" (Acts 2:44-45).

What a marvelous description of family! And yet this description seems to elude us in the twenty-first century. Our individualism has all but assured that family is understood in terms of seclusion and isolation, not connectedness. Our tendencies to protect our clans and families make it difficult for us to envision and enjoy the full inclusion of the family of God.

Decades ago Dr. Martin Luther King Jr. noted that the most segregated hour of the week in America is Sunday morning. Although strides have been made toward a deeper inclusion and vision for the church, Sunday morning is still very much segregated. It is rare, though there are shining examples to the contrary, to find a congregation that is fully inclusive. And yet the Holy Spirit is at work in and through the church. God is not finished with the family. God has not yet finished turning us into the household of God.

> GOD HAS NOT YET FINISHED TURNING US INTO THE HOUSEHOLD OF GOD.

The First Family

One of the most frustrating aspects of the Bible—at least for those who read it—is the long genealogies frequently encountered. Students typically ask, "Why are these lists of names here? Why are they important?" In fact, most people simply gloss over these genealogies; they are regarded as fluff or just a list of difficult-to-pronounce names.

Genealogies are found throughout the Hebrew Scriptures, and in the New Testament we encounter them in Matthew and Luke, and as a spiritual genealogy in the book of Hebrews. For some reason these lists of names were important to the biblical writers.

The reason? Family. Or more to the point, the genealogies exist to demonstrate how important the family of faith is to God. But these lists do not merely record flesh-and-blood connections but spiritual ones. The point the genealogies seem to make is twofold: (1) God has always been at work in our human relationships that span generations, and (2) God works in our human relationships even though they are broken, imperfect, and often impure. In other words, these are grace-filled memories. God has not abandoned the human family. If we want to be assured of this fact, all we have to do is remember our ancestors. Just as God saw them through life, so he will sustain and encourage us by grace as well.

Genealogical research is very popular today, and those who pursue this hobby quickly ascertain that their flesh-and-blood relations are a mixture of kings and paupers, of heroes and villains, of leaders and underachievers. Friends who have traced their own family ties back through the generations attest that they are related to both crown heads of Europe and slave traders, to pastors and prostitutes. Every family is a mixture of great discovery and enormous disappointment.

The same is true of the family of God, and that's entirely the point of the gospel of grace. The biblical genealogies remind us that our spiritual heritage is not a neatly wrapped progression of faithfulness and purity. The family of faith is both a cause for celebration and a case for judgment. Our spiritual families, or our respective faith traditions, can't hold up under the intense scrutiny of the past. We all have our pogroms and problems, our dictators and scalawags. And yet God has not given up on us. The biblical narrative is filled with stories of imperfect people who were offered grace that they might experience a relationship with God.

We dare not make family, weak as it is, an idol. Such idols will fail. God wants to offer the world deeper relationships. These are not flesh-and-blood connections but spiritual ones born of love and grace. This is the family of God.

In the third century AD, many Christians took up a life of community and prayer in the remote regions of Syria and Egypt. We call these people the desert fathers (although there were women and entire families too). These simple hermits adopted a lifestyle of sharing, work, prayer, and play that informed many of the later movements and orders in the church. They called each other "sister" and "brother," and many of their teachings are preserved in the form of parables and legends of the saints. Their community was one of acceptance and concern for the whole, not just for the individual believer.

One of the parables of the desert fathers reveals how these early ascetics felt about the family. To them family was a community of people who cared for each other. But it was a difficult achievement. As this parable shows, building the family of God is a noble but difficult undertaking.

> A brother came to Father Mateos and asked, "What shall I do? Whenever I am among people I cannot seem to control my tongue. I speak out of turn, I condemn people for their good deeds, and I contradict them constantly. What am I to do?"
>
> The old man gave this answer: "If you cannot control yourself, you need to get away from people. Go live alone. Those who live among people must be round, not square. They must be able to turn toward others instead of away from them."
>
> "But you live alone," the brother pointed out.
>
> "Ah, yes," said the old man. "But I live alone not because of my virtue, but because of my weakness. Those who live among people are the strong ones."[2]

So often, we discover the truth of these words for ourselves as we reflect on our own family with our various strengths and weaknesses. Indeed, we should never think too highly of our families, for everyone is dealing with one crisis or another. Broadening our concept of family does not harm us but opens us to new possibilities. We will even discover that when we embrace God's kingdom work as our primary calling, our individual families become part of God's family. We are adopted into God's household.

Not long ago I was reflecting on my own nuclear family and giving thanks to God for our blessings and for the creature comforts we enjoy, the love shared in our home. But I was also mindful that my family is imperfect. As I was praying, I happened to notice my congregation's pictorial directory lying on the coffee table in front of me. I picked it up, riffled through the many photos of families in my congregation, and I knew that these people were part of my family too. In fact, I realized that many of the deepest spiritual experiences of my life had been shared with some of these other individuals. I noted that I had also shared deeply personal conversations with many of these people during times when they had been the most vulnerable or had experienced some amazing blessing or enormous sorrow. I knew I was blessed to be a part of others' lives. I was blessed to be a part of the family of God.

Having grown up in America, my concept of family has often revolved around the nuclear family. But in other cultures, family is much broader. My African sisters and brothers hold to a much broader idea of family, which includes grandparents, aunts and uncles, cousins, and others who live under one roof.

These concepts of family certainly critique our Western idolatry of the family and our narrow view of the church. Family is much larger than we imagine. After all, the followers of Jesus are adopted into the household of God.

I am thankful for this adoption. We are called to create and recreate the family of God in our time—to be bridge builders and healers. It is a great time to be alive, in spite of so many challenges and so much brokenness and bloodshed. It is a great time to hope and to build the family of God. So many people long for love, for real and abiding relationships. Loneliness and despair are so prevalent. This is why our vision of the family of God is so vital. Being adopted into God's family, and seeing others as brothers and sisters, makes all the difference.

Four

THE POWER OF ONE OR
THE POWER OF THE ONE

*"My grace is sufficient for you, for power is made perfect
in weakness." So, I will boast all the more gladly of my
weaknesses, so that the power of Christ may dwell in me.*

2 CORINTHIANS 12:9

*He has shown strength with his arm;
he has scattered the proud in the thoughts of their hearts.
He has brought down the powerful from their thrones,
and lifted up the lowly.*

LUKE 1:51-52

THE EXPLORATION OF DEADLY VIRTUES would not be complete
without delving into the corruption of power so prevalent in our
time. Without careful consideration we often find ourselves em-
bracing power that does not come from God but from our sense
of entitlement, position, or desires. At first blush it might seem
that corrupted power would be easily recognizable, but this often

is not the case. Power has a tendency to hold us captive in its spell or make us act on our worst fears and impulses toward the goal of self-preservation.

From the outset it would also be helpful to consider how power—and our conception of it—are frequently attached to our theology or our understanding of God. For example, Christians and Jews alike have always associated the creation with God's power. While we speak of being caretakers or stewards of God's creation, we also affirm that God alone can create stars and planets and living things. Many of the psalms speak of God's power—the big picture type of power—that awakens our sense of awe: "The heavens declare the glory of God; the skies proclaim the work of his hands" (Ps 19:1 NIV).

In other words, we often associate the greatest power with God. We might even say that this creative power *produces awe*, especially as we consider what God has done and can do. But this sense of power not only fills us with wonder, it also provokes questions of much deeper variety, questions about good and evil and suffering, and God's intentions for us. And yet people of faith always draw back to the idea that God is good, that God's creation is good, and that this ultimate power resides with God alone.

In grade school I memorized the famous poem "Trees" by Joyce Kilmer, which speaks to the power of God and the wonder and joy found in ordinary things.

I think that I shall never see
A poem lovely as a tree.

A tree whose hungry mouth is pressed
Against the earth's sweet flowing breast;

A tree that looks at God all day,
And lifts her leafy arms to pray;

A tree that may in summer wear
A nest of robins in her hair;

Upon whose bosom snow has lain;
Who intimately lives with rain.

Poems are made by fools like me,
But only God can make a tree.[1]

Yes, we associate power with God's creative work, but we also associate power with what God has accomplished through the life, death, and resurrection of Jesus Christ. This is a different type of power, however. The Gospels and the apostle Paul's epistles have much to say about this powerful redemptive work that was accomplished through seemingly weak methods—suffering, death, sacrificial love. We often overlook this power, but it is nevertheless the power of God. It is also the type of power that we can easily corrupt, especially in the church.

Consider, for example, how easy it is for well-meaning people to be seduced by powerful people or by those who tout various forms of power through financial blessings, position, or fame. In our current political and social situation, we might conclude that the Christian faith is about having the loudest voice, holding the highest position, getting the most votes, or having the largest budget or bank account. We could conclude that the best Christians are those who have the most power or prestige. We want the representatives of Christ to be articulate, good looking, electable, and wealthy. In short, we want exemplars of power.

Strength and power have always been seductive for people of faith, especially in times when fear or trepidation is on the rise. And whether it be political or personal, there is always the temptation to place our strength in ourselves or others ahead of God. Likewise, strength—which can be associated with other virtues, such as strength of character or strength of faith—can also become myopic or self-centered without the counterbalance of being aware of our weaknesses and sins (our need).

It seems this has always been the struggle in the church. We struggle with the same lust for power and prestige as the first disciples did. Mark's Gospel, especially, makes a point of recording these struggles.

> [Jesus and the disciples] came to Capernaum; and when he was in the house he asked them, "What were you arguing about on the way?" But they were silent, for on the way they had argued with one another who was the greatest. He sat down, called the twelve, and said to them, "Whoever wants to be first must be last of all and servant of all." (Mk 9:33-35)

> James and John, the sons of Zebedee, came forward to him and said to him, "Teacher, we want you to do for us whatever we ask of you." And he said to them, "What is it you want me to do for you?" And they said to him, "Grant us to sit, one at your right hand and one at your left, in your glory." But Jesus said to them, "You do not know what you are asking." (Mk 10:35-38)

WE WOULD MUCH RATHER BE IN A POSITION OF POWER THAN BEHIND THE SCENES. WE WOULD PREFER TO BE THE BOSS.

These episodes—found in all four Gospels in various forms—reveal a power struggle Jesus addressed many times and in various ways. We too have a strong desire to be first, to be the person with the most influence, to lead by virtue of position rather than by virtue of service and humility. We would much rather be in a position of power than behind the scenes. We would prefer to be the boss.

Likewise, the apostle Paul's writings reflect Jesus' understanding of power and our struggle to create our own forms of salvation and redemption.

In Paul's letter to the church at Philippi, a magnificent hymn describes the difference between God's power and our need. While we often try to exploit God for our own gain or accolades, Paul describes what true power is: humility and servant leadership. The apostle Paul noted that Jesus embodied this servant leadership:

Let the same mind be in you that was in Christ Jesus,
who, though he was in the form of God,
did not regard equality with God
as something to be exploited,
but emptied himself,
taking the form of a slave,
being born in human likeness.
And being found in human form,
he humbled himself
and became obedient to the point of death.
(Phil 2:5-8)

In Jesus we see servant leadership rather than the exploitation of power. The apostle even has the confidence to say that we should be of "the same mind" that was in Christ: power embodied through faith in Christ's work, power not of our making but of God's.

Perhaps, as much as anything, reality TV has contributed to these modern sensibilities about power. We discover we have an affinity for those who have outwitted, outworked, outlasted, or outsurvived others in the group. We love winners. We love leaders. But we often don't see the underbelly of authority or the allure of power that can accompany it.

We also have the tendency to make power an individual pursuit (or achievement). At no other time in history have humans made so much of famous pastors or religious leaders. The Internet and wide swaths of media have given Christians powerful voices on television, in publishing, and even in politics and business. We now live in a time when certain Christian leaders can exercise enormous power over people. And these voices do not always draw the church's attention to the power of God but often to the personalities themselves.

If there is legitimate power to be exploited in the church, the gospel tells us it is the power of the Holy Spirit, which is often manifest in humility and service to the church. If there is power in our faith, it resides in our witness to the grace of God, what God has done through Christ.

Powerful Witnesses

Dietrich Bonhoeffer (1906–1945), a Lutheran pastor and professor who was arrested and ultimately executed by the Nazis for his resistance to Hitler, wrote many texts from prison. His books *Ethics* and *The Cost of Discipleship* have become modern Christian classics. Another Bonhoeffer title, *Life Together*, speaks to the nature of Christian community, both in practical terms and as a power that can overcome the horrors of war. In *Life Together* Bonhoeffer notes that "Christianity means community through Jesus Christ and in Jesus Christ. No Christian community is more or less than this."[2] These are simple and yet profound words. Bonhoeffer makes it clear that the power of the church is not found in individual pursuits but in faith that defines the community—faith in Jesus.

Bonhoeffer also uses an analogy early in his book to shatter our small or petulant dreams about church. He makes it clear that our dreams for the church are not necessarily God's dreams, and God saves us from making the church our own by giving us hindrances and pressing us to survive. Obviously, Bonhoeffer's theology was impacted and tempered by his own individual experience of suffering, but his theology draws the church back to the power of God and forbids us from thinking that the church can survive on our own terms.

Bonhoeffer's powerful description allows us to clearly see that the church is established on the grace of God, and is not of human origin or effort.

By sheer grace, God will not permit us to live even for a brief period in a dream world. He does not abandon us to those rapturous experiences and lofty moods that can come over us like a dream. God is not a God of the emotions but the God of truth. Only that fellowship that faces such disillusionment, with all its unhappy and ugly aspects, begins to be what it should be in God's sight, begins to grasp in faith the promise that is given to it. The sooner this disillusionment comes to an individual and to a community the better for both. A community which cannot bear and cannot survive such a crisis, which insists upon keeping its illusion when it should be shattered, permanently loses in that moment the promise of Christian community. Sooner or later it will collapse.[3]

This accurately describes the church of our time too. It describes what the church needs in order to discover the source of our power. The prevailing winds of individual faith, theologies of wealth and reward, leadership achievements and earmarks, and church growth built on the shaky foundations of our own visionary dreams will not last. Bonhoeffer would refer to such human dreams as the church built on sand (see Mt 7:24-27).

The church is not built on strength in numbers but on the power of God to sustain it.

A friend reminds me of this every time he returns from his work in the Democratic Republic of Congo. For more than a decade he has engaged in mission work, in community work, alongside the pastors and other leaders in that nation. Church growth there is clearly tied to the ability and willingness of people to suffer alongside one another. In the aftermath of war that destroyed millions of lives, the church is thriving because it has not lost sight of its strength, which is its reliance on God.

The Lord said to the apostle Paul, "My grace is sufficient for you, for power is made perfect in weakness" (2 Cor 12:9). The greater danger for the church is that we will not recognize God's power in our weaknesses. Instead of recognizing God's strength, we might come to believe that human power—in all of its varied forms and manifestations—is sufficient. But when our foundation is limited to our own abilities, strength becomes a deadly virtue.

A beautiful proverb states this idea as follows: "Trust in the LORD with all your heart, and do not rely upon your own insight" (Prov 3:5). There is great power in recognizing our limitations, as long as we place our faith in the power of God. Power doesn't come from within us but from God, who made heaven and earth.

The church does not exist to give witness to our own power but to God's. If there is any power to be celebrated in the church, it is not the power of individual achievements but the power found in Christ's living body—the church—which is a witness to the love of God and his redemption of the world.

Again, the apostle Paul, in particular, writes eloquently and comprehensively on these church matters. He speaks often of the need to pray for each other, to share, and to build a true community of care (see 1 Cor 1:10; Eph 4:1-7; see also Acts 2:44-46). The power of the church is not individual but communal.

When the apostle Paul was trying to describe this to the church in Corinth, for example, he used the analogy of the human body. "Indeed, the body does not consist of one member but of many," Paul wrote (1 Cor 12:14). The apostle goes on to describe the strength of the body, not in individualistic terms but as shared power, which is manifest as concern.

> The members of the body that seem to be weaker are indispensable, and those members of the body that we think less honorable we clothe with greater honor, and our less respectable members are treated with greater respect; whereas our more respectable members do not need this. (1 Cor 12:22-24)

The potential of the church is not found in the power of a few but the strength of the many. When all are valued, respected, and offered opportunities of service—along with equal expectations and demands—something wonderful happens in the body of Christ.

My current congregation experienced this power of God—this power of community—some years ago. Immediately after the Vietnam War ended many Vietnamese families fled their homeland via makeshift boats and rafts. Two of these families eventually found their way to the Midwest, to the small town of Brownsburg, Indiana. When people in town learned of the plight of these Vietnamese refugees, families from the Methodist, Lutheran, and Catholic congregations came together to provide for their needs. Homes were opened. Childcare was provided. Jobs were secured. And in time these families found security and a future in America. But this was not the work of one person or even one family, but of many people reaching out in concern and service. There was strength in numbers. The power of God was manifest through faith and action.

These Vietnamese families enjoyed success in America, eventually became citizens, and some of their children became valedictorians of their class and went on to achieve even greater things as engineers, doctors, and public servants. But their meager beginnings in America were brightened by the love and concern of many faithful people.

It is important to remember that we can achieve more working *together* than we can achieve through solitary effort. Many hands are more powerful than a few. And when people come together in think tanks and other creative efforts, marvelous outcomes are wrought from sharing ideas—one idea building on another.

During the months when I was writing this book there were many humanitarian crises around the world. First and foremost among these was the Syrian refugee crisis in Europe. As thousands fled from their war-ravaged land seeking sanctuary and safe haven for their families, it became apparent that parts of Europe would be flooded by these refugee families.

In response the pope issued a challenge to the Catholic parishes of Europe, requesting that each parish consider welcoming a refugee family. Such a challenge, of course, would not be effective on an individual basis, but with many people working together to make a difference to one family perhaps the words of Jesus could be fulfilled: "Whoever welcomes one such child in my name welcomes me" (Mk 9:37).

These are difficult times, and the solutions to human crises are even more complex. But while individuals can feel overwhelmed by these needs, disasters also reveal the incredible strength found in communities, in people coming together to achieve a common goal. The strength of the individual is not nearly as great as the strength of the many. In the book of Ecclesiastes we find this truth repeated in proverbs:

> Two are better than one. . . . For if they fall, one will lift up the other. (Eccles 4:9-10)

> Though one might prevail against another, two will withstand one. A threefold cord is not easily broken. (Eccles 4:12)

These ancient ideas can be applied powerfully to the church. They speak of unity, of persuasion and affirmation, rather than power of the individual. While we often pine after the power of position or prestige, here we find strength in humility and togetherness. Perhaps this is why Jesus' final prayer for the disciples was specifically about unity (Jn 17:21). Christ knew that the church would rest on the power of the Holy Spirit, not on individuals exercising their respective opinions and authority. The church does not exist through our powers but through God's power.

CHRIST KNEW THAT THE CHURCH WOULD REST ON THE POWER OF THE HOLY SPIRIT, NOT ON INDIVIDUALS.

Sometimes, we can confuse the two. In our modern-day haste to lift up the power of the one (the impact of our individual choices and responsibilities) we often lose sight of the power of the One! When we do this, power becomes a deadly virtue. But when we find ourselves grabbing onto this deadly type of power, it is helpful to draw back into the gospel, in which God's power is made perfect through our weaknesses.

The Power Of Weakness

In his book *Choose Love Not Power: How to Right the World's Wrongs from a Place of Weakness*, Tony Campolo dissects the Gospel account of two Jesuses. The first Jesus, the one the church calls Lord and Savior, was Jesus bar-Joseph, or in Hebrew "Jesus the son of Joseph." The other Jesus, as noted in the Gospels, appears soon after Jesus is tried and sentenced to death. The Roman governor Pontius Pilate gives the people the choice of sparing one life. He can either release Jesus bar-Joseph or Jesus bar-Abbas (Barabbas)—in Hebrew, "Jesus son of the Father" (Mt 27:16).

Campolo notes that the differences between these two Jesuses could not be more pronounced. On the one hand we have Jesus of Nazareth, who was born in the small, out-of-the-way village of Bethlehem, who grew up in a no-account village of Nazareth, and who preached that the meek would inherit the earth (Mt 5:5). Jesus also taught that his sacrificial death was for all of humanity and that he would draw others to himself through a place of weakness on the cross (Jn 12:30-33). He said that his kingdom was not of this world or of its powers (Jn 17:16), and that the weapons used by his followers would not be the weapons used by this world (Mt 26:52; see also 2 Cor 10:3-4).

The other Jesus (Jesus bar-Abbas) noted in the Gospels obviously believed and practiced a different philosophy of power. He had been arrested as a murderer (a knife or a sword was his weapon of choice), for insurrection against the state, and for inciting others to follow his lead. This Jesus was intent on wresting power from the Roman authorities, and he practiced his views by staging guerrilla attacks against Roman soldiers and inciting others to take up the sword of power.

Campolo notes well the differences between these two Jesuses, who may have even grown up together or known each other. But the deeper question, like the one posed to the religious authorities of the first century, will always be, *Which Jesus will you follow?* Will we seek the powers of this world or commit ourselves to following the path that Jesus of Nazareth took, lived, and taught? Extremes, yes. But an important choice nonetheless.

Power—even seeking power—often produces disastrous results. And usually these results are not so clearly evident in the lives of those who seek it, but are more prominently displayed in the lives of those on the receiving end—the powerless. Power is often mad. It is often not easily recognized until it is too late and others suffer.

To put it another way, the strength we seek from God is often made ineffective through our lack of faith. We often discover, as we consider our motives and our desire for power, that we are frequently motivated by fear. True power comes from God, and if we heed the vision of the prophet Isaiah, we learn that God

> **POWER—EVEN SEEKING POWER—OFTEN PRODUCES DISASTROUS RESULTS.**

> gives power to the faint,
>> and strengthens the powerless.
> Even youths will faint and be weary,
>> and the young will fall exhausted;
> but those who wait for the LORD shall renew their
>> strength,
> they shall mount up with wings like eagles,
> they shall run and not be weary,
>> they shall walk and not faint. (Is 40:29-31)

There is marvelous power in faith—power we frequently look past, just as those first followers of Christ sought their own positions of power and fame. We often grab for what is easy to obtain, thinking this is the power of God. And this is often expressed in the church as power in numbers, the accolades of others, or even the fame or fortune that comes with being a "successful" church leader or media personality. It's natural for us to take an easy road to power rather than seeking God's power.

As I consider my own path through thirty-five years of pastoral ministry, I realize that I have made frequent rest stops among some of the more alluring arcades of power. There have been times when I have sought power (though not always being aware of my motives) in the forms of position, salary, or even the gratitude of others. I have at other times become controlling, overtly opinionated, or even overly critical of others—all forms of power and control that have at certain times landed me in "good stead" in the eyes of the world. At others times, though, they have brought me to my senses and helped me return to my first faith, which is relying on God's grace and authority.

Power in the church can be an insidious beast.

Being aware of these power plays can also save us from much hardship and heartache. The 2016 Academy Awards awarded best motion picture to *Spotlight*—a film dedicated to addressing the sexual abuse scandal that had rocked the Catholic Church some years ago. These scandals, and the sexual abuses visited upon many young men and women in the church, provided a glimpse into how ecclesiastical power can go awry. The powers afforded to priests and pastors must never become abusive, and clergy must always be on guard against them. These powers are not always evident, but are sometimes subtle and persuasive in seemingly innocuous forms.

POWER IN THE CHURCH CAN BE AN INSIDIOUS BEAST. Likewise, secrecy and the spiritual control of others are two of the most deadly forms of ecclesiastical power evident today. When leadership is not transparent, either in conversation or decision, power can become abusive and people can get hurt, especially the young and the vulnerable.

As such, leaders in the church must be on guard against these abuses and also expose them to the light when they do arise (and they do!). Those entrusted with authority in the church—whether lay or clergy—must embrace God's power rather than seek it for themselves. God's power resides in humility, unity, and love. Our weaknesses, when exposed to God's amazing grace and love by faith, reveal the power of God.

It is not our power that makes the difference but the power of the One!

Powerful Endings

Through the years I have seen many wonderful expressions of God's power at work in the church. And like many others I have also witnessed destructive forms, even abuses, of power in the church.

Some years ago a clergy colleague and good friend found himself at the wrong end of power in his congregation. Although he resigned from his position, citing abuses of power—decisions he had made that had harmed others and their reputations—he found healing later in a humble approach to ministry. He discovered that he was most grateful for God's grace to forgive, a "most powerful" and transformative realization. It was only by the grace of God that he was able to exchange one power for another, that he was able to lay aside his own lust for power to embrace God's redemptive power.

These stories are not uncommon in the church—and they point us to the ultimate need that we all have for God's grace. We so easily forget this. *Our* forms of power do not transform. God's power does, which takes us back to the awe of God's creative work, which is an interior power, the work of transforming the human soul.

For millennia there have been stories of *our* powers given up to embrace God's redemptive power. Though they are ancient, they are ever new for our time. Such is the case with the story of a young man, Francesco, who lived in the Middle Ages. Born and raised in Italy, Francesco ("the little Frenchman") grew up as a fun-loving youth; he enjoyed affluence and all of the desires of his heart. As he would explain later, he outdid all of his contemporaries when it came to vanities and enjoying the desires of the flesh. At one point Francesco left home to fight in a bloody skirmish with a neighboring city, where he was taken as a prisoner of war.

This experience as a prisoner, followed by a year-long convalescence back home, brought Francesco to his senses. Living as a hermit beside the crumbling walls of a church in San Damiano, Francesco heard the voice of God in the bells, a message telling him, "Rebuild my church!" Francesco followed this voice, literally and figuratively, first by rebuilding the walls of the church edifice, and then by becoming the spiritual leader of a new movement to repair the soul of the church.

Francis, as he would later be known, exchanged forms of earthly power for God's power through love of and service to humanity. He gave lavishly to the poor and took a vow of poverty, becoming completely dependent on God. He organized new communities around the simple disciplines of prayer and daily sacrifice—the power of God's grace. Those who witnessed Francis, his sister Clare, and the others invested in this new spiritual community commented that they were people "wrapped in humility, focused on God through contemplation and invested with power from on High."[4]

In many respects Francis sought to return the church to its first love, which was trusting in God's power. Francis sought to live as the church had lived in the first century (see the book of Acts).

Since that time, many other movements, reformations, and revivals have also called the church back to this power of God, this redemptive grace. We don't have to read very deep or very long into church history to find other voices, other witnesses, calling the church back to a deeper trust in God's power.

Martin Luther, a sixteenth-century church Reformer, spent much time writing and speaking of these very things. "Here I stand," said Luther, his conscience captive to the Word of God. This became one mantra of the Reformation period, and in tow with this singular idea was a faith that stood on the grace of God, the ultimate power to reform and transform. Luther's progression of ideas was not new, but he was able to articulate many wonderful metaphors that spoke to faith as the ultimate power in our lives.

Once, Luther said, "If Christ were coming again tomorrow, I would plant a tree today."[5] This is an astounding view of hope, and we can salute the grandeur of this strength in Luther's broader vision of God's power when he wrote:

This life is not righteousness but growth in righteousness.
It is not health, but healing. . . .
This is not the end—it is the road.[6]

There are indeed many roads we can take in life. Some of them lead to powerful forms of destruction, even in the church. Others lead to powerful forms of life. God help us to choose wisely.

THE LURE OF SUCCESS OR
THE ALLURE OF GRACE

Blessed are the meek, for they shall inherit the earth.

MATTHEW 5:5

AFTER BEING ACCEPTED TO THE DUKE DIVINITY SCHOOL IN 1982, I headed to Durham, North Carolina, with a full head of steam, a new Oxford annotated Bible, and eighty dollars in my pocket. I was excited, anxious, and eager. I was also dead set on becoming a great scholar, and my vision for my life was littered with excellence and all of the trappings of success.

But that bubble soon burst.

I quickly discovered that while I had proficiency for languages and Bible, I had to work very hard at my studies. The hours spent in seclusion—hunkered down in the bowels of the library reading mounds of books—were turning me into a hermit. My struggles in academia were further exacerbated by my work in parish ministry, where I had, surprisingly, discovered that people appreciated my sermons, my teaching, and my insights. People in the congregations kept telling me, "You are so good! We need more good pastors like you!"

For some months I actually believed all of the nice things people were saying about me. (This is a problem for *all* pastors.) Fortunately, I was saved from these accolades while sitting in the university library one afternoon. That day, deep in my studies and my sermon preparation, I happened to glance up at the magazine rack and noticed a colorful magazine bearing the auspicious title *The Wittenburg Door*. Taking the magazine from the rack and flipping through its pages, I discovered page after page of satirical exposés on the church and religious leaders. The magazine had a particular humorous slant, especially toward those in the religious world who seemed to regard themselves as important, successful, or saintly. In essence, I saw myself being exposed by the satire, and I immediately wanted to write for the magazine.

That desire came full circle a few months later when I was contacted by then-editor Mike Yaconelli, who invited me to submit my own brand of satire to the magazine. We became regular pen pals—mostly through the editorial help Mike provided early on—and in time I became a regular contributor to *The Door*. But more importantly, Mike saved me from a life of overblown self-importance. He helped me to see that "success" and "goodness" (especially when one is talking about ministry) is a sticky wicket—a trap that religious folks can easily fall into. Mike provided a long-distance friendship and a forum to discuss the pitfalls of religion, especially in matters of the heart, where our concepts of righteousness, holiness, or even goodness can become means to their own ends.

Mike spoke of, and wrote about, these matters often. And yet he was able to maintain a humble life through service. He often said he served the "slowest growing church in America" during a time when church growth and increasing numbers were the earmarks of success, fame, and fortune for some church leaders. Although he died too soon (in an automobile accident in 2003), Mike had a great deal to say about the false gods of success, but more importantly, he actually lived humbly and eagerly cast aside those "virtues" that so easily lift a religious person onto a lofty pedestal of admiration.

I have never forgotten Mike's path of service and the sense of humor he brought to the life of faith. Mike understood the meaning of success, and he worked diligently to expose those attitudes and personalities that were more worshiped than worshipful. There is a difference, as we will see. The golden idol of success can be most unnerving, especially when we realize this virtue is detrimental to a life of humility and faith.

This is especially true in our time, when success and all of its trappings infiltrate the life of faith so easily. Success is one of the most widespread desires of our time. But with a bit of exposure, we see that success is not the same as faithfulness. It's often a far cry from it.

The Allure of Success

Success is one of the greatest allures of our time, even in the church. It's particularly powerful because we now live in a time when so many outcomes are associated with failure, such as poverty, unemployment, or depression. Or we value success so highly that we can scarcely see how struggle, perseverance, or faithfulness might produce greater longterm results in people and institutions.

For example, consider how these images of success (and failure) influence our attitudes and decisions when it comes to education, faith, business, or family.

- Schools across the nation are now graded via the results of test scores, where some schools (teachers and students) are given *A* ratings and others are regarded as failures.

- In sports—even youth leagues—winning is the ultimate goal. Values such as sportsmanship, integrity, and learning fundamentals are often cast aside in the pursuit of success.

- Politicians often describe another candidate's character, history, or track record as *successful* or *a failure* instead of speaking to policies or issues.

- *Success* is more commonly defined in economic terms (wealth) than any other way (e.g., development of intellect, skills, helpfulness, or excellence).

- A congregation's or pastor's success is most commonly described in numeric terms (members, budget, attendance, square feet) rather than spiritual terms (discipleship, faithfulness, service, or outreach).

Of course, these are mere sketches of common attitudes toward success, but if we take the time to consider them more specifically, I believe we would discover that our ideas of success are deeply personal. In fact, if we are honest with ourselves, I believe we would discover that these attitudes drive many of our decisions and actions. Our drive to "succeed" enters into our discussions with children (and affects their decisions), our marriages, and the workplace. It is often difficult to know where our idea of success came from (Is it godly?) or what outcomes we hope our success will produce (a more faithful follower of Jesus?).

In short, we are in a quandary when it comes to success. We want it. We want to be defined by it. But we don't know how it fits into the Christian faith, or whether success is the same as or different from being faithful, generous, or a disciple of Jesus.

Our view of success migrates into our attitudes about goodness, power, and generosity. We like the idea of success and would rather be associated with it instead of failure, but we can't quite arrive at a place where success fits neatly into the gospel of Jesus or helps us in our struggles and sins. Deep down, we know we are sinners saved by grace, but there is something more satisfying about the notion that we are successful and don't really need God's help. After all, sin implies that we have failed. And we don't like the idea of needing God. We'd rather be self-sufficient and self-made. In a word, successful.

I have come face to face with these demons many times in my life. But I have not always recognized them.

During the years I was serving as a student pastor in North Carolina, I know I struggled mightily to be seen as a success. I was told—in direct conversations as well as through insinuation—that my ministry would be affirmed and rewarded based on certain outcomes or achievements. For example, while the church didn't have an organized youth group, my success with the teenagers brought many accolades. And when it came time to raise money for missions, my success in fundraising produced a corresponding increase in my salary.

I enjoyed these early successes and the favorable comments from parishioners, but deep down I knew these successes could not become my motivation for ministry. I learned that I could produce results, but I realized that much of ministry could not be measured by these standards of success. I felt torn between the many unseen and immeasurable aspects of ministry, such as prayer, study, counsel, friendship, and confession, and the more public expressions of ministry that people noticed, such as preaching, teaching, administration, and corporate leadership. On the one hand I longed to spend more time in reflection and prayer; on the other I knew that people commonly graded me on the outcomes I produced—a growing budget, confirming and baptizing souls, increased membership.

This tension has been around for a long time, not just for pastors but for all Christians. What is success, really? How far and how fast do we push for results? And if Jesus called us to make disciples (teach, preach, baptize [Mt 28:19-20]), then how does this yardstick of success differ from being faithful to the call, or does it?

Some years ago I was assigned to mentor a middle-age colleague who had entered pastoral work as a second career. During our sessions together, I would frequently hear stories about his former work in the business world, where he felt that he was constantly under the microscope of success. If his sales numbers didn't continue to increase, for example, his boss would chastise him for being lazy or ineffective. And when his sales numbers led the company, he would be rewarded with bonuses, certificates of achievement, and special recognition.

"Neither of these responses were an accurate portrayal of the realities of business," he once told me. "I felt equally devalued as a success and as a failure, and neither outcome described the real value I thought I was producing. In the end I felt I had to leave those ideas of success and failure behind. I was unhealthy. I developed an ulcer. And though I went out 'on top,' I knew that it was all based on numbers and not anything that could be measured under the microscope of integrity, friendship, or fidelity. I thought ministry would offer me a different set of values and measures."

But my friend discovered that this was not the case.

"Success in the church just gets mixed with a different color of Kool-Aid," he told me. (This conversation was just a few months after the Jim Jones tragedy.) "Bishops and parishioners still want pastors to produce numbers—but of a different variety. Instead of talking about sales figures and prospects and increased profits, I'm now asked to increase my apportionments to the conference, increase worship and Sunday school attendance, and bring new families into the church."

I've had many such conversations since, and many Christians can speak to these frustrations and attitudes that creep into our discipleship. Of course, we do want to make disciples, we know that a congregation needs a solid budget, and we don't want to lapse into laziness or a devil-may-care attitude that makes all outcomes meaningless. But we also want to remain faithful and hopeful, especially in those times when the struggles seem to outweigh the outcomes, when perseverance is required over power or the prestige of impressive numbers.

But these are also age-old struggles. And we can see these struggles embodied in Jesus himself. Consider the apostle Paul's beautiful tribute to Christ and his own definition of success. These scriptural affirmations do not always correspond to our modern definitions of success, and in fact, they challenge them.

About Jesus, Paul says,

> Who, being in very nature God,
>   did not consider equality with God something to be
>   used to his own advantage;
> rather he made himself nothing
>   by taking the very nature of a servant,
>   being made in human likeness.

> And being found in appearance as a man
>> he humbled himself
>> by becoming obedient to death—
>>> even death on a cross!
> Therefore God exalted him to the highest place.
>> (Phil 2:6-9 NIV)

About himself, Paul says,

> Whatever were gains to me I know consider loss for the sake of Christ. What is more, I consider everything a loss because of the surpassing worth of knowing Christ Jesus my Lord, for whose sake I have lost all things, I consider them garbage, that I may gain Christ. (Phil 3:7-8 NIV)

Wow! These affirmations of "success" certainly challenge our contemporary ideas. In light of the gospel, success is defined not as something we have done but what God has done in Christ.

> IN LIGHT OF THE GOSPEL, SUCCESS IS DEFINED NOT AS SOMETHING WE HAVE DONE BUT WHAT GOD HAS DONE IN CHRIST.

Toward that end, let's make yet another attempt at seeing success through new eyes.

What Is Success?

The life of Christian faith is not built around *our* definitions of success, whether individually, corporately, or theologically. Rather, Christian faith is firmly grounded in the success of Christ, namely, his triumph over sin and death. Therefore, whatever we are trying to accomplish is done in his name, for his honor, and for outcomes that will bring glory to God and not to ourselves.

But even though we know the gospel, arriving at these attitudes and outcomes remains difficult. We see these successful attitudes in ourselves, hear them in the accolades and portrayals of others, and even despise them at times when they are clothed in the grandiosity and pomposity of politicians, celebrities, or the worship of wealth and position. They are always with us, and they challenge our faith. They are a challenge to the church, perhaps now more than ever before in human history.

Success is our personal pursuit. The ends we seek are often success oriented.

Not long ago I noted this struggle during a march organized by a church federation. This march through Indianapolis was offered as a proclamation of hope and justice, lifting up the voice of peace in crime-riddled and violent neighborhoods. The march was also organized as a means of bringing the church together, offering a new vision, a "face," in the hope that it would foster deeper dialogue about race, poverty, and social inequality. At the beginning of the march, however, one leader warned of being lured by success.

"The march itself is not the success," she said. "Just bringing black and white together is not success. Success will only be recognized when there is no more violence in the streets, when all of our children have hope, when we can worship together without recognizing our race first but rather see Christ in each other."

I had to say amen, and I also realized that gospel success is difficult to submit to, for the gospel is submission to God's will in Christ. That day, as I marched for peace in the streets, I kept wondering, *What is my role in pointing to the ultimate reign of God? Where might I need to change in order to embrace God's work more fully?* That would be success according to the gospel.

We rarely measure our personal successes in this way. I have always felt this tension. And I also see the tension played out in our many definitions of success in the body of Christ. I am convinced that when we become confused about the gospel definition of success (God's work in Christ), we also see many forms of coercion, frustration, and burnout among laypeople and clergy alike.

In *Leaving Church*, Barbara Brown Taylor describes her varied frustrations in the Episcopal priesthood and the unfolding events that led to her "compassion burnout." Her decision to leave the parish priesthood for a teaching post at Piedmont College was, as she describes it, also about the confusion she was feeling about people's expectations and her ability to fulfill them. She is not the first to arrive at this place in ministry, nor will she be the last.

Taylor's story is not about the superiority of the priesthood versus teaching or about the superiority of certain gifts in ministry. But she hints at the contemporary expectations of success Christians often place on themselves—or that Christians place on each other—as much as it addresses the core of the gospel, which is that we are not able to build ministry or the church on our own foundations of success.

Through the years I have had many conversations hinting at these frustrations and inclinations toward burnout. In most cases, this burnout is built around our own definitions of success or the successes portrayed via the business world, through sports competitions, or even power struggles. I have also encountered them in myself.

The truth is, when we don't stand on the grace provided through Christ and in the power of the Holy Spirit to make all things possible, we often come to believe that the church hinges on our own efforts and achievements. We set ourselves up for disappointment, if not failure. And when something doesn't go right, or when people don't buy into our vision, or when there are financial or spiritual struggles, that is when ministry can fold like a house of cards.

Likewise, when a congregation approaches a pastor, or sees the work of the pastor, as primarily being about producing, earning, or achieving, disappointments are bound to occur. Or the pastor simply works to death until he or she discovers that there is never enough compassion to go around, never enough time, never enough energy to meet the ever-expanding set of expectations and goals. When this happens, God's grace is no longer at the center; our human efforts and expectations are.

Success becomes yet another deadly virtue.

What we need is not more effort, not more success on our own terms or success built around the expectations of others, but a renewed awareness of God's victory offered as grace. This is where power comes from as well as purpose, meaning, and a healthy (spiritually healthy) definition of success.

WHAT WE NEED IS A RENEWED AWARENESS OF GOD'S VICTORY OFFERED AS GRACE.

During the days when I was writing this chapter, I too struggled with these definitions of success and grace. I was blessed to be given a special gift by my congregation—a gift of grace—that helped me to find clarity during my final years in ministry and build a more healthy definition of success.

I was granted time overseas to travel to Spain and walk the Camino de Santiago, the centuries-old way of St. James. This pilgrimage offered me an opportunity to leave behind the trappings of ministry, even the successful trappings of marriage, family, and technology. I stripped myself of all creature comforts (no cell phone, no regimented meals, no showers, no expansive wardrobe) and made a covenant to experience each day, each moment, as it came. I would walk the way in prayer, in reflection, as a way of seeking God and his path for my life. I would do my best to take no assumptions with me on the pilgrimage, but would continually ask three questions along the way:

- God, what would you have me experience today?
- Lord, where would you bid me go when I return?
- Master, what would you have me do in my final years of pastoral work?

These questions guided me along the way. I tried to remain open to relationships, conversations, and chance encounters that might reveal God to me. I forfeited my expectations, traveled light, kept my eyes open, my heart willing.

The pilgrimage of the Camino became a journey into God, and I soon learned that I had to let go of my old view of success. As I walked, I became aware of the grace that had covered my life and ministry. Life, the church, even ministry itself was not about me. It was not about success. It was about relationship. Relationship with God. Relationship with others—my family, my friends, and those who were yet to embrace faith. I sighed many sighs of relief. It was not about me! The church was not being built on my gifts, labors, and accomplishments. The church was built on Christ and his love and his triumph over sin and death.

I did not feel successful on the Camino. I felt blessed. I felt enormous gratitude. I was continually in awe, at times each day close to tears, when I considered the depth of love God has for the world in spite of our brokenness and decay. Seeing my life in this crucible of divine love, I was blessed to be a part of God's triumph, not my own accomplishments.

I returned from the Camino with a newfound sense of joy and gratitude. My purpose in life did not change, but my focus did. Some of my first love for ministry returned. I was able to leave behind the old trappings of success and embrace the church and service to humanity with new, healthy energy. I was thankful to God.

I am not saying that I have this figured out. I am not saying that I have arrived or have all of the answers. But the Camino did give me a new awareness (or a refreshed awareness) of what success really looks like. Sharing Christ and his love is success. Living in Christ and his love is success. All else pales by comparison.

Final Thoughts

There is a famous story (perhaps apocryphal) about Mother Teresa appearing on a television talk show. When the host asked Mother Teresa about her successes working with sick and dying people in Calcutta, she replied, "We are not called to be successful. We are called to be faithful."

The Gospels are replete with numbers. Jesus fed five thousand, including women and children. He preached to multitudes. He called the Twelve. He sent the Seventy in pairs to minister to dozens of villages.

My own Methodist tradition is shot through with this same infatuation with numbers, record keeping, creating goals, and speaking of ministry in terms of figures and statistics. In and of itself, this discipline is not a bad thing. Numbers do have a tendency to keep ministry honest, to cause us to reflect on the outcomes of our work and our vision. I don't know of any tradition or tribe in the church that does not use numbers to shape its hopes and dreams, its needs and deficiencies, its attendance or stewardship. No church-related schools ignore numbers related to students enrolled, budgets, and the ranking or successes of alumni and professors (teaching effectiveness or publications). No church-related institutions ignore the configuration of human needs and the way these needs are met in terms of personnel, budget, or outcome.

However, the church must take care that facts and figures do not eclipse our purpose and call. Sometimes numbers lie. Sometimes numbers, especially "successful figures," make us complacent in our discipleship or entice us to affirm our own achievements rather than God's grace and power. Likewise, numbers that may reflect failure do not necessarily indicate a lack of faithfulness. Some facts and figures can also reflect changing times or new challenges. They can be the cause of celebrating God's faithfulness in the midst of lean times. After all, not all of the psalms are about giving thanks for blessings and successes. Many are about giving thanks for God's steadfast love in the midst of hunger, danger, or even dire circumstances. We would scarcely call, for example, the twenty-third psalm a "Psalm of Success."

Success has become a siren call in our time. It is assumed that if we are not a success, we are a failure. We often assume that if a congregation is not producing a certain number of disciples, growing a budget, or sending out scores of missionaries, then that congregation is a failure. Likewise, universities and church-related institutions can often get more traction comparing themselves to public institutions rather than affirming their core values or traditions. Our definitions of success are often more closely aligned with big business or professional sports than with the gospel of Jesus. But success, as defined by the gospel, is affirming that our futures are in God's hands and that our faithfulness is what God seeks most of all, along with our recognition that his grace abounds far more than our earthly successes ever could.

WHEN GOOD ISN'T GOOD ENOUGH, GOD IS STILL GOOD

As he was setting out on a journey, a man ran up and knelt before him, and asked him, "Good Teacher, what must I do to inherit eternal life?" Jesus said to him, "Why do you call me good? No one is good but God alone."

MARK 10:17-18

OF ALL THE VIRTUES ASSOCIATED WITH CHRISTIANITY—*goodness* may be the one most commonly expressed. Christians are supposed to be *good* people. Christians do *good* works.

As such, goodness is often regarded as the goal of the Christian life. We might even say that most Christians long to be good. And we certainly enjoy it when others call us good. That's a *good* thing, isn't it?

Perhaps. But let's have a deeper look.

A few years ago, during a European vacation, my wife and I spent several days in London. One morning, while walking across the Thames, we happened upon a rather inconspicuous building directly across the street from Westminster Abbey. It was the

Methodist Central Building—and much to my surprise and delight, a large throng of neatly clad clergy were milling about on the lawn. Being a Methodist myself, I ambled over and began conversing with these brothers and sisters, and I learned that they were Salvation Army clergy (officers) who were gathered for their annual conference.

I told one group that I was a Methodist pastor from the States and then asked, "What associations do people in England have with the Methodists? How are Methodists in England regarded by the English people?"

One gentleman answered, "There aren't nearly as many Methodists here as there are in the States, but the people of England regard Methodists as good people who do good work."

There was *the* word. Hearing it actually filled me with a sense of pride, made me glad to be a Methodist. But as I thought about the response later, I began to wonder, *Why goodness? Why not faithfulness? Holiness? Or humility?*

Not that goodness is a bad word, but I realized that there were some virtues that could become just a byword, an innocuous, limp virtue devoid of real meaning or significance if left outside of the gospel.

After all, I had encountered these realizations much earlier in my life.

During my first years of pastoral work I was fortunate to enjoy the friendship of a seasoned ministry pro who became my mentor. His name was Paul, a retired pastor who lived across the street from our cracker-box parsonage. Though we were generations apart, Paul became a dear friend, and I found his company endearing and demanding. He was at once gracious and forthright, even as he was affirming and honest. Mostly, I appreciated his insights about ministry.

One afternoon, while we were sitting in a restaurant having coffee, Paul asked, "So, how are you *really* feeling about ministry?" I was always comfortable in Paul's confidence, so I opened up and shared from my heart. I told him about my "successes" and my frustrations. I also told him that some people gave me accolades while others seemed to think I was a bum.

"That's the problem with leadership," Paul said. "The greatest temptations we all face in life have to do with what we are hearing about ourselves. I've learned that both ends of the spectrum are false. We should never believe those people who think we are the greatest thing since sliced bread. And we shouldn't give too much weight to negative opinions either. It is helpful to remember that we don't stand or fall on our own goodness. Regardless of what people think, we always move through life with integrity, which is having a balanced and honest opinion of ourselves."

I have never forgotten Paul's beautiful sentiments, and there have been many times when I have taken his words to heart. We don't have to be good. We just have to be faithful.

Although a difficult virtue to address, our concepts of goodness can have a dark side, especially when it comes to faith in God and our need

> WE DON'T HAVE TO BE GOOD. WE JUST HAVE TO BE FAITHFUL.

for God's grace. In fact, Jesus himself addressed this dark side at various junctures when he interacted with the religious leaders of his day (commonly noted in the Gospels as the Sadducees, Pharisees, and scribes). Time and again we see how "good" people—who regarded themselves as defenders of the faith or protectors of the law—failed to grasp their need for God's goodness, or failed to see God's image and goodness in others. In short, the high pursuit of being good (and in most cases being right) was more akin to building walls than building bridges, and the ultimate need for God's grace was simply rejected or overlooked.

Take, for example, the Gospel accounts of the rich young ruler. Here, a young man approaches Jesus seeking (we learn in due course) an off-handed approval of his well-to-do and successful life. But the young man masks his hope in a question: "Good teacher, what must I do to inherit eternal life?" (Mk 10:17-22; see also Mt 19:16-30; Lk 18:18-30).

Jesus notes the young man's wealth, his worldly successes, but first responds, "Why do you call me good? No one is good but God alone." (In Matthew's Gospel Jesus' response is recorded as, "Why do you ask me *about* what is good?"). Centered in Jesus' response, however, is the recognition that the young man has an inflated sense of his own importance, of his own goodness. And when the young man indicates that he has kept all of the commandments, Jesus asks him to give his wealth (his successes) to the poor. The young man is shocked by this request and goes away saddened, perhaps, most notably, because Jesus refused to recognize how good he truly was, or, perhaps, that he was at least *good enough*.

Here we see the dark side of the virtue of goodness: the idea that our various successes, achievements, awards, honors, and accolades somehow amount to something in the eyes of God. Goodness, as a virtue, can sneak up on us that way. First, we regard ourselves as good enough, then accomplished, and then outstanding, and finally indispensable. Before long we don't need anything from God or anyone else. We have arrived on our own merits.

A quick glance through philosophy can also help us in this assessment of goodness. The Greek word used in the Gospels here—*agathos*—is an old word that dates back to various Greek philosophers and their respective philosophies. These Greek ideas, even in first-century Galilee, were very much at play in the Roman world. In its various nuances the word *goodness* drifts into more refined ideas centered on excellence, and in certain philosophies of the time it came to mean "pleasing to the gods" or even "salvation." In other words, the pursuit of goodness was regarded as the highest goal and was the one thing all enlightened people should seek. Our modern concepts of goodness have not trended far from these ancient moorings, and we don't have to go far to find them at play today, even in the church.

We catch a glimpse of this predicament (namely, our desire to be good while trusting in the grace of God) throughout Paul's epistles. But Paul always makes a distinction between the goodness of the believer and the goodness of God, noting that the goal of faith is *to receive* the goodness of God, which is our salvation and the way of life made *possible* through grace (see Eph 2:8-10; Col 1:10). Goodness, in Paul's theology, is not a virtue for the believer to admire, depend on, or hoard for self-benefit, but is the goodness of God at work within us: "I am confident of this, that the one who began a good [*agathos*] work among you will bring it to completion by the day of Jesus Christ" (Phil 1:6).

Goodness, as noted by both Jesus and Paul, is not a virtue deriving from within us or that distinguishes us from

> WE ARE NOT SO MUCH GOOD AS *BEING MADE* GOOD.

those who are "not good," but rather, good is what God *makes us* through grace. Goodness is the work of the Holy Spirit. We are not so much good as *being made* good. And our goodness is never something to be touted as the defining aspect of our lives. Rather, both Jesus and Paul regard the higher virtues of humility and kindness as the *inward* and *outward* expressions of any goodness we possess.

I must confess that I always feel a certain thrill (dare I say, elation?) whenever someone notes how "good" I am, or how much they appreciate all the good I do for the church or the community. I much prefer these accolades over criticism or other acknowledgments of my deficiencies (of which I have many). Nevertheless, sometimes it feels "good" to point out my deficiencies to others, thereby creating a stir as others recognize the depth of my amazing humility.

What a vicious cycle!

But these thoughts and experiences so often hearken back to some inflated sense of self, to the notion of goodness that we harbor so carefully and so pridefully in the church. Of course, it is much easier to spot these tendencies in others rather than in ourselves, which is another thing about the virtue of goodness: it is often judgmental.

I have encountered this many times, and so have you.

Some years ago I recall feeling very good about the formation of an interfaith event I had worked diligently to organize. I was elated when leaders from the Jewish, Muslim, Christian, Mormon, and Hindu faiths agreed to come together to provide both an overview of their respective beliefs and an opportunity for people to ask questions in a respectable and honest conversation (or so I hoped). But after the first hour it was apparent that this would not be the outcome. I was embarrassed when some of the worst offenders, the most disrespectful, were Christians. One lady continued to point out the superiority, even invincibility, of the Christian faith. Part of her diatribe contained the idea that Christianity created good people, and God knows the world needs more good people! And likewise, her attitude and theology suggested that other faiths produced "bad" people. And God knows we don't need more of *them*!

Of course, in that setting it was impossible to point out the discrepancies and mistakes posed by both the woman's attitude and her representation of the Christian faith as ultimately being about "goodness." But her thoughts, I am afraid, are representative of many in the church today.

This attitude has worked its way into the church in many forms. It is often noted, and even defended, as being somehow essential to the protection of the Christian faith. The attitude seems to be that if we can't be better than others, if we don't possess the superior faith, then what is the point of believing?

Much like the story of the rich young ruler in the Gospels, our personal attitudes toward goodness can affect us deeply. This virtue tends to rear its head whenever (and maybe *wherever*) there is tension with the grace of God, especially in situations where we are prone to build ourselves up or point out the failures of others, thereby marking us as "the good guys." This virtue remains all the more difficult to identify because it is ingrained in our Christian DNA. The pursuit of goodness is part of our human tendencies; most people hold a higher opinion of themselves and their beliefs than they do of others and their beliefs. Goodness can, in essence, become like the scales of judgment. Goodness tells us who the good people are, while bad people languish in failure and frustration.

"Goodness" may even be part of our human condition. And it can influence our spirituality.

We have a difficult time, for example, praying certain prayers, especially in the household of faith. We have a tendency to relegate certain prayers to select seasons, when it is necessary to recognize our brokenness. Otherwise, we may not need God. We have arrived. Unlike the psalmist, we tend to regard ourselves as good instead of recognizing our need. But let's look to Psalms as our guide.

There is no one who does good.
The LORD looks down from heaven on humankind
 to see if there are any who are wise,
 who seek after God. (Ps 14:1-2)

There is no one who does good.
 No, not one. (Ps 53:1-3)

Although these are our human tendencies, the psalmist also recognizes the goodness of God. And there are far more expressions of God's goodness to be found in these prayers.

Answer me, O LORD, for your steadfast love is good.
 (Ps 69:16)

For you, O Lord, are good and forgiving,
 abounding in steadfast love to all who call upon you.
 (Ps 86:5)

For the LORD is good;
 his steadfast love endures forever,
 and his faithfulness to all generations. (Ps 100:5)

[The LORD] is good,
 for his steadfast love endures forever. (Ps 107:1)

O give thanks to the LORD, for he is good;
 his steadfast love endures forever. (Ps 118:1)

The LORD is good to all,
 and his compassion is over all that he has made.
 (Ps 145:9)

This latter psalm is certainly identified with Jesus, who taught that his heavenly Father showed mercy to all—as God alone is good. Jesus expressed goodness in terms of love and forgiveness when he said, "Love your enemies and pray for those who persecute you, so that you may be children of your Father in heaven; for he makes his sun rise on the evil and on the good, and sends rain on the righteous and on the unrighteous" (Mt 5:44-45).

There is goodness that can lead us to God and goodness that can lead us to believe we are self-sufficient and privileged. The former is life. The latter is a deadly virtue.

> THERE IS GOODNESS THAT CAN LEAD US TO GOD AND GOODNESS THAT CAN LEAD US TO BELIEVE WE ARE SELF-SUFFICIENT AND PRIVILEGED. THE FORMER IS LIFE. THE LATTER IS A DEADLY VIRTUE.

Works and Goodness Redefined

When the Pilgrims landed on the shores of the New World, they brought with them not only their desire for religious autonomy and all of their worldly possessions, but also a pronounced theology of self-reliance, right living, and the idea of salvation as evidenced by wealth, wonders, and success through hard work. We call this the Protestant work ethic, but it is so much more. This theological mindset has deeply influenced the church in America.

That is not to say that the Pilgrims (or the Puritans) were a bad lot. Far from it. There was a bold righteousness in their thought and a preconceived goodness in their steps. They certainly believed in their way and dared not veer too far from the path they perceived would lead to life.

The early Puritan work ethic continues to persevere in much of Christian thought, especially in America. In our culture we are far more likely to build a bridge from our own sense of goodness to God's mercy, rather than the other way around (that is, God's mercy creates the possibility of our doing good). God is good, yes. But let's not get carried away! Look at what we have accomplished!

Before this theology of accomplishment invaded our American history, a similar mindset appeared in the history of Israel, which is preserved in the Bible. Scholars call it the "Deuteronomic History," which has to do with the second expression of law and the new attitude reflected in Deuteronomy ("second law") and in portions of Judges, 1-2 Samuel, and the two books of Kings. In these Scriptures we find a theology built more around personal responsibility and the pursuit of goodness. Failure, in Deuteronomy, is not so much disregard for the Torah as the inability to ascend to personal righteousness and doing the right thing.

Perhaps this is reflected in the question posed to Jesus by the rich young ruler, or perhaps it was reflected in many of the religious leaders of Jesus' day. Keeping the law was *doing* good and caused a person to *become* good. But Jesus questions this. Is goodness really something we can attain?

If we are honest with ourselves, we would likely admit that doing the right thing is never easy. And seeking the right thing is complicated all the more by life's struggles and challenges. Often, in our pursuit of goodness, we can inadvertently harm others or their ability to find answers. So, our own goodness and right answers can get in the way of helping others.

Perhaps this has never been more true than in mission work.

Not long after the earthquake that rocked Haiti in 2010, thousands of well-meaning Christian organizations descended on Haiti. To date, billions of dollars have been poured into that tiny nation, but there is little difference today than in the days following the quake. There are many reasons for this, of course.[1]

To be sure, graft, bureaucracy, limited resources, disease, and overwhelming poverty have all played a role in Haiti's unchanging landscape. But the desire to "do good" has also contributed to Haiti's continued struggles. Having talked to many mission teams who have returned from Haiti, I have found shared frustration in the inability to make headway. People go to Haiti to make a difference, but the results don't seem to be evident despite the billions of dollars and the thousands of volunteers.[2] Why?

Often, good people get in the way of each other. Sometimes the good people who go to help are themselves consuming the resources and energies meant for others. (It takes food, shelter, and energy, after all, to provide for this army of workers.) And sometimes our "doing good" for others inhibits or prohibits the recipients from doing good for themselves or making their own decisions. Instead of providing a hand-up we think we are doing more good by providing a handout. But handouts do not remove the source of the need, making it essential that another group follow our group to meet the same need. Likewise, those who go to "do good" often come home feeling good about their efforts even though nothing has changed for the poverty-stricken Haitians.

One Haiti volunteer summarized this conundrum well: "It would be much easier and more effective to remove all of the inhabitants from Haiti, bomb all of the cities down to rubble, and start over. And it would probably be less costly too. I've never seen a situation where so many people come to do good, but depart feeling that they have done no good at all."

Goodness has a way of being elusive and insidious, and it often creates waves of joy in us while creating nightmares for others. As one of my missionary friends often notes, "It's difficult—but

Christians need to stop trying to do good *for others* and begin to listen *to others*. The answers—and the proper questions—rarely reside in those coming from the outside to fix a problem in another nation. The answers most often already reside in the lives and the resources of those who are on the inside of human misery."

GOODNESS IS WHAT WE EXPERIENCE IN COMMUNITY WHERE LOVE AND COOPERATION BECOME THE DEFINING MARKS OF THE CHURCH.

Goodness is not a fix or a spiritual gift. Goodness is what God makes us by grace. Goodness is what we experience in community where love and cooperation become the defining marks of the church.

Whatever Happened to Grace?

Somewhere along the way we seem to have lost our concept of the goodness of God's grace. In Philip Yancey's book *Vanishing Grace: Whatever Happened to the Good News?* he addresses this conundrum in compelling ways.

Today, as Yancey notes, we are more apt to hear a sermon about changing our behaviors, becoming better people, or doing good than to hear a message about God's grace revealed in Jesus. Much theology today (especially what we hear on radio and TV) is berating or belittling others, with Christians being the winners and everyone else the losers. If there are sins and difficulties for Christians to overcome, the prevailing thought seems to be that Christians can choose rightly by their own willpower, without any help from God. There is no grace needed—just decision and effort, or perhaps proper counseling. Who needs the grace of God when we can create a church built on proper beliefs and hearty, self-reliant Christians who will take control?

It often appears that the concept of grace is missing from the church. Many today cannot tolerate weakness or need in the Christian community. Goodness is enough. The church seems to be the only army in the world that shoots its own wounded. We don't need grace.

I have been blessed to encounter grace in unexpected places. In fact, that's what makes grace so amazing. It's not limited to the hallways of the church. Some years ago, during a youth mission trip to Denver, I had taken a small group of teens to a local shelter and soup kitchen. We spent much of the day cleaning showers, scouring pots and pans, mopping floors, washing bed mats, and hosing down sidewalks. By the end of the day we were tired, hungry, and feeling good about our efforts.

During the day, however, we had also taken the time to talk to the shelter's residents. We encountered many bruised and broken lives. Some of the men in that shelter spoke openly about their struggles and the decisions or circumstances that had led to their life on the streets. We heard, of course, many stories about alcohol and drug addiction. We heard stories about legal troubles, broken marriages, and strained relationships. We also heard about health problems, military disabilities, and larger issues that eroded their lives over time. Sadly, some of the men had mental health difficulties and could not express how they felt.

At the end of the day some of the teens reflected on what they had heard. "Some of these men just had a bad turn," said some. Others pointed out that certain men in the shelter were not so unlike a father or a brother they knew, but these men's lives had migrated in different directions. Some wondered what would have happened if they had made different decisions or had experienced favorable breaks at key junctures in their lives.

Out of these reflections, many of the teenagers were able to articulate grace in a new way. "We're more alike than not," one teen said. "We all need God's help to make it through. It's just that we are all struggling with different issues."

On the way out of the shelter that day, we passed by a hand-written sign that one of the residents had written on a piece of poster board. It read: "I'm not what I should be, I'm not what I could be . . . but thank God Almighty, I'm not what I was."

Grace. The forgotten word.

Although we often look past this need in our lives, it is important that we pause in grace to take inventory of our concept of goodness. We would all do better with the former (grace) than the latter (goodness). In grace we find community and forgiveness. In goodness we often find judgment and criticism. Or we discover an inability to raise ourselves to the levels of goodness we would like to exhibit.

We so easily forget that life is a struggle, that we stand in need of God's strength and goodness to help us in our weakness. While we may enjoy the idea of being good (or perhaps being better than others), this does not lend itself well to the formation of Christian community—the body of Christ. This body is fashioned in God's grace, not our goodness. And the body that Paul describes in 1 Corinthians 12 is more closely aligned with displaying our varied needs than celebrating or lifting up our indispensable gifts. No one becomes good without God's grace. And the church doesn't work without God's forgiveness and love at the center.

In her 1991 novel *Saint Maybe*, Anne Tyler explores some of these themes. Her story centers on a young man, Ian Bedloe, whose disastrous meddling leads to his brother's suicide and his sister-in-law's death. Plagued by guilt, Ian assumes the care of his niece and nephew (as well as his ailing parents). He is torn by his desire to fulfill his family obligations and his desire to have the freedom of a young man.

One evening Ian wanders into a small church—the Church of the Second Chance—and becomes friends with the pastor. Ian makes a life for himself among the kind and generous people who welcome him. He is never the same. He discovers in the church that life is about second chances—and even third and fourth and seventy-times-seven chances—and that God's grace is enough for him to care for his little family and even learn how to be a son, and father, and friend.

Tyler's beautiful story awakens us to the reality of grace and helps us glimpse the beautiful possibilities that are within our grasp. We are not perfect, and we are not good enough, but grace *is enough*. And when we awaken to God's presence in our struggles, we discover that all things are indeed possible with God's help. Our goodness won't get us there. But God can.

The Scriptures don't hide these realities from us either. They are always there, lurking beneath the surface of many a narrative.

Take the story of Jacob, for example. Here is a young man whose name (in Hebrew) literally means "the one who grabs." That is young Jacob in a nutshell. He grabs (steals actually) his brother Esau's birthright and blessing. Jacob takes most everything that does not rightfully belong to him. He is a trickster and a grabber.

We can readily identify with the young Jacob. We too find ourselves with insatiable appetites. We often get what we want, only to want more. And frequently, when we obtain one goal or blessing, we are not satisfied but immediately desire another and another and another. Consumption becomes our addiction. We simply want, and we can't even say why.

Later in Jacob's life, however, we see how God's grace extends a new life to Jacob (Gen 32). By the River Jabbok, Jacob meets a mysterious stranger who wrestles with him until dawn and eventually puts his hip out of joint. But Jacob prevails, and out of his struggle he is given a new name: Israel. The name literally means "one who struggles with God."

There are many lessons here. But one that we should not miss is that we are called to struggle with God. Life is a struggle, and out of our hardships and pain we have many questions. But we must question, continue the fight, and seek to prevail. Faith is not about having the answers but staying in the fray. Faith is not about being good but wrestling through life's difficulties until we reach the dawn and receive a new name, a new identity, by the grace of God. Faith involves struggling with the One who is greater, knowing full well that we may be hurt, but that through our many questions and burdens we may receive a new life and a new direction.

After his struggle, Jacob—Israel—was reconciled to his brother Esau, returned to the Promised Land, and became one of the patriarchs of the nation of Israel. Nothing was possible without God's grace, and nothing in Jacob's backstory would lead us to the conclusion that he was a "good" man. He was not good; he was transformed.

Once we get a glimpse of God's amazing grace, we discover that our goodness is not of our own making. Goodness, when we attempt to define it for ourselves and our own ends, can be a deadly virtue. We may even discover that goodness fails us. Grace never does.

Two More Brothers

There may be no greater illustration of these disparities than the parable Jesus told about the two brothers, the so-called parable of the prodigal son (Lk 15:11-32). This parable, which we explored earlier in the introduction, has many nuances and a depth of meaning.

Jesus tells the story of a younger son who asks for his inheritance from his father. He subsequently travels to a far country where he squanders everything. When he comes to his senses, he realizes that his only option is to return home and beg his father's forgiveness. On his way home, while he is still a long way off, the father sees the son, runs to meet him, and welcomes him home with a banquet feast that includes the fatted calf.

Hearing that his father has welcomed home the prodigal, the older brother flies into a rage. He chastises his father, pointing out his own faithfulness and superiority. But the father notes that while he always has the older son, he must welcome the younger home. "He was lost," the father says, "and is found," "dead and is alive again."

A very powerful parable, to be sure, but one that does not linger long on the minds of the faithful. As one fellow noted after we shared this parable in a Bible study: "This story isn't fair. What kind of father would actually do this?"

God would. And God does.

This parable demonstrates, in part, the difference between the righteousness of the good and the righteousness of the forgiven. The former value goodness as a self-prescribed virtue. The latter value the goodness of the Father, who creates good outcomes through grace. These theological disparities are all the more evident in our culture today. Many value goodness as its own end. Others see goodness as a gift of God, who is the giver of all good gifts.

When we explore goodness more deeply, we sometimes become troubled by what we see. Our values pale in comparison to God's grace.

Years ago, when my grandfather was still among us and offering his sage wisdom, I recall an event that helped me to see this truth more clearly. My cousins and I had been playing on a sand pile when a small skirmish ensued. Feelings were hurt, words were exchanged, and tears were shed. But as we gathered around our grandfather, each one of us wanting to be right and attempting, over the higher volume of the others, to be heard, he silenced us with a gentle word: "Of course, someone is right and someone is wrong. Someone acted first and someone else retaliated. Others joined in and took sides. But if you are going to be a family and get along on the sand pile, you are going to have to put those differences aside and forget about them. You are going to have to forgive. I can tell you to stop fighting, but I think you would rather learn how to work out your differences while you are having fun. How about it?"

Though each of us was hurt in our own way, we all agreed with our grandfather's wisdom. And that was that. As I recall, the rest of the afternoon was pure joy and without incident. By the time we went to bed, all was forgotten and the world was right.

This is a great place to leave this chapter on goodness. Yes, we can strive to be good. But when we fail in our attempts—as we inevitably will—it's good to know that forgiveness trumps the lot. And grace is sufficient.

Seven

GENEROUS TO A FAULT OR OVERFLOWING WITH GRATITUDE

*So whenever you give alms, do not sound a
trumpet before you, as the hypocrites do in the
synagogues and in the streets, so that they may be
praised by others. . . . But when you give alms, do
not let your left hand know what your right hand is
doing, so that your alms may be done in secret; and
your Father who sees in secret will reward you.*

MATTHEW 6:2-4

AMONG THE DEADLY VIRTUES, generosity is one Jesus noted on several occasions. This deadly virtue, so common today in a culture that craves recognition and reward, has drifted into the church in numerous ways. In many respects generosity (or being recognized for one's generosity) is one of the most alluring virtues in the church. Being recognized for one's generosity is part and parcel of most stewardship campaigns, for example. And sometimes pastors or financial campaign consultants publicly recognize key donors, large financial contributors, or top gifts. Generosity is such an integral part of most preaching and teaching that it is sometimes difficult to differentiate between faith and showmanship, between faithfulness and "success."

Generosity is an especially insidious virtue because concepts of faithfulness and reward have infiltrated the church, most notably through the so-called health-and-wealth theologies of many prominent TV preachers. Their theology espouses reward for generosity. As one TV preacher announced: "If you give a hundred dollar gift to this campaign, God will bless you tenfold. What are you waiting for?" But we cannot blame TV personalities alone for this corrupted theology of generosity. It surely existed in Jesus' time too (see Mk 12:41-44; Lk 11:42). And it is quite prevalent in today's congregations. I know that I have personally been guilty of certain sly approaches to fundraising (as I have received expert coaching from those who raise funds for a living). After all, if I am going to ask others to give, then I need to make it clear that I am contributing a large gift too.

Perhaps you have noted this quandary of generosity in yourself. Although money is a necessary component to ministry, we typically dislike talking about money—even though Jesus talked about money a great deal. Our difficulty may arise from our need for praise and recognition rather than our need to give. Or we may eschew talking about money because we keep most of it for ourselves and our own purposes, giving out of abundance rather than out of sacrifice.

Many stories in the Gospels call attention to these difficulties. One such story is found in Mark.

He sat down opposite the treasury, and watched the crowd putting money into the treasury. Many rich people put in large sums. A poor widow came and put in two small copper coins, which are worth a penny. Then he called his disciples and said to them, "Truly I tell you, this poor widow has put in more than all those who are contributing to the treasury. For all of them have contributed out of their abundance; but she out of her poverty has put in everything she had, all she had to live on." (Mk 12:41-44)

Here we see the deadly virtue of generosity on full display. Giving in the Jerusalem temple was a public affair, often completed with trumpet fanfare and cheers when the top givers stepped forward and their huge sums of silver or gold were dropped noisily into the treasury bowl. Jesus, of course, notes these large gifts, but he is not impressed. Rather, his gaze fastens upon a poor widow whose gift does not warrant any fanfare. In fact, the gift is so small that others may have simply turned away or scoffed at the insignificant sum.

But this is a story about generosity and misplaced generosity. It still speaks to us. It is a story that calls out the disparities between *how* we give and *why* we give. It reveals hidden motives.

Generosity is a virtue that can cause us to look past the source of our blessings, which is, of course, the Lord. The one great temptation of generosity is to see ourselves as the source of the gift rather than seeing the Giver of all good things. We often give without recognizing that God's work—God's generosity—makes our generosity possible.

I have experienced these struggles many times in my life and have seen them in others as well. When I was a young seminarian I completed a summer internship working alongside a seasoned pastor who, upon arrival in this parish, was immediately pressed to complete a capital campaign initiated by his predecessor. At one point in the campaign I was present at a board meeting in which one gentleman made it clear that he was against the proposed building campaign and urged others to vote against the building plan (which had been discussed and supported for years). He was the only dissenting vote, and the plan was carried forward with great enthusiasm by the others on the board.

After the meeting I asked my mentor to explain what had just happened. He said, "I often find that the people who are the most vocal *against* using money for God's work do not themselves *give* to God's work, and they don't want others to accomplish the work lest they be exposed for their lack of generosity." I have found this to be true in many cases since. Generosity is one virtue that can be built on many foundations. We give because we want a tax write-off, because we want recognition, because we like the idea of giving, or because God first gave his Son for the redemption of the world (Jn 3:16).

As Jesus noted, God sees the realities of our generosity because God sees our heart.

There are many reasons why we might give, not all of them related to the gospel. And sometimes we may even find that our generosity draws attention to those who do not or cannot give much. Church history is replete with these examples.

Some years back, when my wife and I were enjoying a tour of early Methodism in New England, we were struck by the many old Methodist churches containing numbered pews. Historically, this dates back to the time when the numbers on the pews represented one's pledge to the church. The family who gave the most sat in pew one, the second-largest givers sat in pew two, and so forth. This practice was at once celebratory and demeaning. Those who gave the most were afforded great privilege and essentially rented the seats nearest the pulpit (and, consequently, were in full view of the rest of the congregation). Those who gave the least were relegated to the pews in the back. This practice was prevalent in the era, not just in Methodist circles but in many others. In time it led to movements that fought this practice. The Free Methodist Church traces its heritage back to the insistence on *free* pews, wary of the deadly virtue of generosity.

Many of these practices are still at work among us in more subtle forms. It is not uncommon to find congregations that affirm large financial gifts and applaud the *largesse* of some while ignoring the *sacrifices* of others.

Recently, a woman in my congregation asked a very insightful question: "When is the last time we recognized someone who has taught a children's Sunday school class for twenty years instead of applauding the person who gives a one-time gift to the building fund?" Indeed! I marvel at such insights and also feel dejected for not having thought of it myself. Generosity is about so much more than money, and gratitude is the key to turning any gift into an expression of faith.

The Attitude of Gratitude

Yes, generosity can become a deadly virtue, but aren't we called to *give*? Isn't the Bible replete with the call to be givers?

Absolutely! And when we delve more deeply into these questions, we discover that generosity calls us to examine our attitudes about our time, talent, and treasure. Without self-awareness, without gratitude in giving, we can lapse into routine; we become people who merely go through the motions of service and generosity. In routine or duty, we can inflate our own sense of self-importance, or we abhor the giving itself. We might even resent God for asking us to give, or even reject God as the Giver of all good gifts.

Once, while planning a stewardship campaign, one of the largest donors noted during a meeting: "I don't know about the rest of you, but I really hate giving money to the church." Although others at the meeting cringed at this honesty, I departed that evening suspecting that many Christians feel that way about their commitments to God's work. We would rather do other things with *our* money. It's so easy to lose our awareness and appreciation of God's abundance.

Hence our quandary. If we lose sight of the gospel—what God has done for us in Christ—we may also lose sight of why we give, why we are called to be generous. In many catechisms, including my own Methodist tradition's Articles of Religion, we learn that we give "because Christ has redeemed us and by the power of the Holy Spirit is creating us in Christ's image, so that we may be grateful for God's goodness in prayers, presence, gifts, service and witness."

Martin Luther, the sixteenth-century Reformer, offered a marvelous bit of theology along these lines. He recognized that we are not made generous all at once. Luther believed that God is always at work within us, calling us to deeper places of faith and commitment. Generosity is one aspect of life in which we are continually being converted to Christ's image. God does not foreclose on us but continues to suffer along with us. We need reminders that God provides, reminders that we are but stewards of the gifts of God.

Luther often spoke of stages of conversion. First, he considered what he called a "conversion of the mind": We are convinced of God's truth and grace, and make an intellectual ascent to faith.

He also spoke of the "conversion of the heart": God's deeper work begins to change our attitudes, our care of and love for others. Here we become more like Jesus, demonstrating that faith is not just a set of beliefs but an active work that moves our hands, feet, words, and actions. And finally, Luther spoke of the "conversion of the purse": We recognize that all gifts come from God, that we do not own our lives or our livelihoods. Everything in life is on loan, even our loved ones, and we are actually stewards (or keepers) of God's gracious abundance.

Some generations later, John Wesley spoke of these same attitudes of faith. Wesley stressed "three simple rules for living"; namely, "Do no harm," "Do good," and "Stay in love with God." A rule attributed to John Wesley's teaching also emphasized that believers should "earn all they can, be as frugal as they can, give all they can, to as many as they can, for as long as they can."[1] These teachings also strike at the heart of misplaced generosity and call forth an attitude of gratitude instead of stinginess or the need for recognition. Humility was to be at the center of doing good.

As I think about some of the most meaningful gifts I have given (and also received), I realize that most of these were anonymous. Whether given or received, fanfare was removed from the exchange, leaving room for the gratitude itself, the joy of sharing with one another. I think this is what Jesus had in mind when he said, "Do not let your left hand know what your right hand is doing" (Mt 6:3). Giving anonymously is tough business, but it's most rewarding when we consider the things of God.

Gratitude affects us immensely. Psychologists pointed out, for example, that when we receive a harsh word from someone, get a bad review, or feel judged in some way, it takes ten compliments to offset that one negative word. This makes our gratitude all the more important, and points out the reasons why we should offer praise to children, to those who work with us, and to friends and family. A word of gratitude builds up and is one of the most generous actions we can provide to others.

Over the course of my thirty-five years of pastoral ministry, I have made a point of keeping affirming letters that people have sent my way. It has served me well. In one corner of my office I keep a box filled with these affirmations. Whenever I am having a bad day, feel the weight of people's judgment, or I am tempted to think that the work is in vain, I read some of these letters. My affirmation box has saved me from despair many times, and I know it would work for you too. Feeling the gratitude of others in word, in helpfulness, in affirmation is an important gift, and it call us to similarly respond to others so the body of Christ may be built up.

Gratitude is the one attitude that can save us from the deadly virtue of generosity. Gratitude removes the emphasis from the gift and places it squarely on the Giver, God. Gratitude restores our faith and removes our pride from the act of giving.

> GRATITUDE RESTORES OUR FAITH AND REMOVES OUR PRIDE FROM THE ACT OF GIVING.

But we have to work at it. Gratitude, after all, does not come easy.

Nevertheless, consider how often the act of giving is accompanied by this saving grace of gratitude. Time and again we find prayers of thanksgiving in the Bible, especially in Psalms. These ancient song-prayers encourage us to give thanks whenever we worship God (Ps 100:4; 147:7) and remind us that gratitude is an act of the heart as well as the hands (Ps 50:14; 95:2).

In every New Testament epistle we also find this attitude. Paul is constantly giving thanks as he remembers those who have helped him or encouraged him (Phil 1:3), and he also gives thanks for other acts of kindness (2 Thess 1:3). We would do well to be people of gratitude, always remembering what God has done. And just as Paul wrote letters to express his gratitude, a written word of encouragement to another person may be worth more than any monetary gift. The work of gratitude—of thanksgiving and thanks-living—should be at the center of our faith and of our attitude toward others.

Often when we speak of stewardship today, we use the phrase "time, talent, and treasure" to indicate how our gifts go far beyond the financial. In fact, God looks at the heart of the giver. God may not desire our financial gifts but right living and action based on sharing the love of Jesus in word and deed. Our time and talent—what we give to God's work in service and devotion—is equally as important as our financial generosity. And we discover that once we have given our lives to God's work, we also desire to give our resources to God's work too. Generosity built on gratitude is the natural outcome of faith.

We need to learn how to receive as well as give—and receive graciously. Not long ago I served on a mission team in Guatemala. Initially, I was apprehensive about this effort, but I soon learned that I had the wrong set of expectations. Instead of giving to others, I first had to learn how to receive from the people of Guatemala. I had to be willing to accept their love, their faith, their hospitality. This was clearly evident in their joy, which, despite their poverty, was infectious. As I used my time and labor, I was receiving so much more. The people gave to me out of their gratitude to God. Gifts poured forth in gracious hospitality, tasty but simple food, and welcoming smiles. Receiving these gifts made me all the more grateful and made my giving a joy rather than a burden. I learned that joy and gratitude are not linked to material things. Those who have little are often the most joyous. And sometimes those who have much are miserable in their relationships, their stresses, and their desire to obtain even more.

Before we can be generous, perhaps we must learn how to receive. "Freely you have received," Jesus said, "freely give" (Mt 10:8 NKJV). Generosity is never built on an attitude of superiority, privilege, or expectation. Generosity isn't self-serving but self-emptying, giving with no expectations of reward or honor. It is an act of faith that requires an open heart and an open hand. When we are open, we can receive what others have to offer too, and many of these gifts we receive are life giving and life changing.

This is a lesson we can learn from the geography of Israel. The Sea of Galilee is continually renewed because it gives. The Sea is the headwaters of the Jordan River, which flows through the country and gives life. Eventually the waters of the Jordan empty in the Dead Sea—which is dead, indeed. This huge body of water, the lowest point below sea level on earth, is stagnant with minerals. Why? Because it does not give. The Dead Sea only receives water, it does not release any. So, while the Sea of Galilee is a life source, the Dead Sea isn't. No life. No release. No giving.

Likewise generosity, if bottled up or removed from the source of gratitude, will eventually dry up, becoming a deadly virtue. Whereas gratitude can give life to both the giver and the recipient, pride and arrogance remove us from the source. Giving as a mere act of duty will eventually dry up or foster the belief that we have created the gift itself through our efforts.

Sometimes we discover that the greatest lessons in generosity are not found in church, but elsewhere.

Renewing Generosity

When we look beyond ourselves and our faith community, we sometimes find refreshing attitudes of gratitude. We might discover that new forms of generosity are emerging elsewhere. And we can learn from these small acts of kindness and helpfulness that seem to elude people of faith.

During the time when I was serving as pastor of a university church, I had the privilege of working with many African students. These students were a marvelous gift to me in many ways. Foremost among these was their friendship, their helpfulness, and their insights. Many were storytellers, and I enjoyed listening to their traditional African tales told over a cup of coffee. One story went something like this.

Two friends, both basket weavers, lived in adjacent huts. Each day the men worked on their baskets, preparing their wares for the busy Saturday marketplace. One afternoon the younger man discovered that he had exhausted his supply of basket handles. *Oh, no,* he said to himself, *What will I do? I have no more basket handles and cannot complete my baskets in order to sell them. I will be destitute.*

Upon hearing of his younger friend's plight, the older man returned to his own baskets and removed all of the handles. He gave all of his handles to his friend and said, "I have extras." In this way the older friend forfeited his own livelihood for the salvation of a friend.

Jesus used many parables that espoused a similar vision of generosity. The parable of the vineyard workers comes to mind (Mt 20:1-16), or the parable of the talents (Mt 25:14-30). These stories, and others Jesus told, seem to address the incongruities of our own resourcefulness and our concepts of generosity as compared to God's greater grace. These parables help us to see how God works through us to create a kingdom of grace and love.

Generosity, when offered in a spirit of caring and love, and not concerned with recognition or fanfare, can have an enormous impact on others.

During my college days I was part of several college ministries that struggled to be present in and offer help to the community. At the same time some campus fraternities were known for their community service (e.g., beautifying roadsides and visiting the elderly). Later, when I became involved in a ministry at the local jail, I was astounded to find that two other men had been making visits for years. These men had been sharing their time and expertise to teach inmates how to read, to mentor them in learning a trade, or just to listen to their problems.

Consider how many people give their time and energy as volunteers in local hospitals, or the people who sit in reading corners in our public schools. Consider how many people give their money and resources to organizations that provide nutrition, mentoring, or assistance to children. Others demonstrate generosity through their involvement in communities across the country. Some businesses give millions of dollars to various charities through grant programs, initiatives, or by matching the gifts given by their employees. The Christian community does not have a corner on the generosity market; many others are doing great work and have carried on without fanfare or recognition. In other words, this spirit of generosity is more widespread than we might think.

Sometimes, we may even see the gospel—God's grace and generosity—in some unsuspecting places. One Sunday afternoon, while my wife and I were having lunch in a restaurant with big screen TVs, I noticed, at the halftime of an NFL football game, that the league was presenting the Walter Payton Award to a player. This award is given annually to honor an active NFL player who embodies the spirit of the late Walter Payton, a Chicago Bears running back. This award is given to a player who has given time, talent, and treasure to his community. It celebrates gratitude and generosity of spirit.

Generosity knows no bounds. Our best work in the church might be found by joining hands with others in the community to address a problem, meet a need, or respond to a tragedy. Over the years I've seen how the church responds to disasters such as hurricanes, tornadoes, fires, and floods. Human crises seem to bring out the best in humanity, forcing us to work together to help friends and neighbors regardless of their race, creed, income, or station in life. Disasters have a way of bringing people together in unexpected ways and perhaps open the floodgates of heaven.

A few years ago, after a tornado swept through several small towns in Indiana—destroying hundreds of homes and leaving great numbers homeless—I noted how folks around the state came together to organize relief. After the trained first responders created a framework for this help, thousands of people (most of them not affiliated with any church or religious organization) began forming work teams and bringing supplies into the area. The gifts given ranged from lumber and hardware supplies to food and bottled water. Millions of dollars were also collected. Homes were rebuilt. Communities restored. And families were reunited.

These tragedies bring people together in new and life-affirming ways. We rarely detect hints of racism, sexism, or concern for nationality or religion when people are working side by side at the site of a tragedy. When we leave behind our ulterior motives, we become generous in the ways Jesus described. Love your neighbor as yourself, Jesus said. Love is the true gospel of generosity.

How we would fare as people of faith if we kept this same spirit of generosity and helpfulness alive throughout the year, and not just in times of disaster? Might this urgency make us more generous, even more kind and loving toward others in the human family? Would the church become less aware of race, sex, and station of life?

We discover in the biblical passages that reveal the amazing generosity of the first-century church that people who care for each other are generous to a fault. When the weakest and most vulnerable people in society are cared for by the church, something amazing happens. We may yet discover how our generosity can be "good news to the poor," "release to the captives," "recovery of sight to the blind," and freedom for the oppressed (Lk 4:18).

Learning to be generous is tricky—especially for people of faith. Shoddy theologies and wrongheaded attitudes creep into the mix. We fall into the trap of believing that our blessings are God's personal reward, or that our displays of generosity somehow impress the Creator. Jesus taught much the opposite. And when we see generosity being lived out by others, perhaps our hearts and minds can be changed for the better.

Generosity as Simplicity

When I moved to Durham, North Carolina, to begin my seminary education at Duke Divinity School, I happened to room with a graduate student from Beijing, China. We became fast friends and have remained so over these many years.

Helping my new friend adapt to American life and culture was a challenge, and we had many late night discussions about the differences between American and Chinese culture, about our families and life experiences. These discussions led me to see our

American way of life through new eyes. I learned, for example, that American life is more fast-paced than life overseas. I also learned that Americans have many more consumer choices, and that these can be overwhelming to those not used to free enterprise.

My friend also helped me to see that our culture is filled with excesses. Most of us live far beyond our means. Many of us live under a cloud of debt to keep up appearances and feed our every desire. This is true not only of individuals but also communities, even churches.

Jesus was speaking to these excesses when he warned of the false virtue of generosity. Living within our means is the greatest form of generosity we could imagine. Learning to live simply, free of excesses and personal extravagance, means we are thereby free to give to our heart's content, making the most of the time. We can trade our self-absorption for helpfulness and extravagant generosity.

Certain Christian communities (e.g., the desert fathers and the Amish) have learned these lessons. Others have followed. We can see through these examples and countless others how simplicity frees us from our prisons of self-absorption and releases us to the joy of giving. Living simply also frees us from debt, from certain overbearing worries, and from various stresses associated with keeping up with the Joneses. Through simplicity we are free to be God's people, free to give and to receive as God intended.

Over the years I have known hundreds of people who have exhibited this style of living. Most of these folks are not paupers, but they have learned the secret to happiness that comes from simplicity and gratitude.

In one of my earliest pastoral appointments I was astounded by the generosity of an older woman who had lived her entire life in a tiny farmhouse on the edge of town. Her entire career had been spent working as a secretary for a large business in downtown Indianapolis. She had no family, was the last of her line, and seemingly had enjoyed no great stream of income during her long life.

When she died, this woman gave her small farm (and tiny home) to the church, asking that it be used as a retreat center or church camp in perpetuity. Right away, some wondered, *Can we afford to keep the gift?* But this dear lady had also given her entire life savings—some $500,000—to make this work possible.

Others asked, "How could she have saved that much?" "Why would she give it all?" or "How is such a thing possible?" It was due to her simplicity, the ways she had lived in service and dedication to others. Her gift was pure faith and gratitude. She wanted no accolades for the gift, no recognition. She simply requested that Christ be honored in the work.

Think of how much is possible when we live a life of simplicity and helpfulness. Generosity as show is deadly. Generosity as gratitude gives life.

This woman's gift, and the testimony of her life, is still bearing fruit decades later. Many have been touched by her generosity, and her life has continued to serve as an inspiration to me and many others who are attempting to simplify their lives.

GENEROSITY AS SHOW IS DEADLY. GENEROSITY AS GRATITUDE GIVES LIFE.

Some years back, while in a doctor's waiting room, I discovered a newspaper article about a wealthy entrepreneur in our community. He had learned the lessons of simplicity through living below his means. He had always made a good living—some might say, an *exceptional* living—but few would have known it. When asked about his philosophy of life, he responded something like this: "Early in my career I made a decision to earn all that I could, but I quickly learned that I didn't need all the things that money could buy. In fact, I was bored by it all. And so I decided I would enjoy my wealth by giving it away, by using it to improve the lives of others. At first I gave a tithe, but as the years went by I continued to give greater and greater percentages of my money. It actually turned into a kind of game. How much could I give? How many people could I help?"

I was struck by this man's philosophy. I hoped that others in the church might attempt to emulate this approach. Toward that end, I have known people who simplified their lives by downsizing their homes, driving older cars, or growing gardens in the backyard. Others have simplified their entertainments, enjoyed more time with family and friends on the pack porch, or simplified their spending habits. As the old adage states: "One never has enough until one knows how much is enough." A life of simplicity offers us this gift. And some people learn the lessons of gratitude in other ways.

A friend owned a large company. At one time, before he sold the company for millions, he had offices in several states, owned a fleet of company cars and trucks, and employed hundreds. One afternoon I asked him about his philosophy of life, and he said, "I've always been grateful for my business. Yes, I'm made a ton of money. But I am mostly proud of the many families I've been able to help by providing jobs and income. In fact, I try to create a work environment second to none, and everyone in the company is valued and affirmed. Family comes first and business second. I hope I can always show gratitude in this way. Everything I have I owe to God, and that is why I give."

Visiting with these friends and many others, I have to wonder if we couldn't use a new word for generosity. We might do well to invent new concepts of giving built around simplicity and gratitude, new ways to be more helpful to our friends and neighbors around us. In fact, how we live should demonstrate the depth of our generosity, not just the size of our bank accounts or the frequency of the checks we write. The Christian life was meant to be a *lifestyle*. And our lifestyle should certainly be defined by generosity in gratitude.

Glad and Generous Hearts

When I was a boy I enjoyed spending time in my father's barbershop in the summer. Perhaps I was infatuated with my father's work, watching him cut men's hair and giving shaves with a straight razor. But seeing how my father went about his business, how he interacted and joked with his customers, had a deep impact on my perception of work as I got older.

Two other businesses were on either side of my father's barbershop. One of these was a shoe store, owned and operated by a very dedicated Christian couple who often gave me small gifts and tidbits of advice. They seemed happy in their work and often mentioned the ways they were engaged in their church and helped support a missionary overseas.

On the other side of my father's business was a shoe cobbler. I don't know if this old-world craft has survived in our throwaway culture, but back then the cobbler was an indispensable partner in restoring worn shoes. This deaf and mute man often repaired our family shoes. He could read lips, but he also carried paper and a pencil in his pocket to communicate with his customers.

At first, I was afraid of this man. However, as I got older I came to appreciate the cobbler and realized that he was a devout Christian man. He always had a smile for me when I brought our family shoes into his shop.

When I was in my early teens, we made a special connection when he realized that I was curious about his business. He demonstrated how he detailed old shoes and restored them with polish and shine. He allowed me to pound a few small nails into the soles of my father's shoes, essentially making them like new again. And at the end of his demonstration he wrote on a slip of paper and handed it to me: "Young man, remember, whatever you do in life, do it for the glory of God."

I've never forgotten this man's simple message and his attitude toward work. He had a simple life filled with dignity and grace. His simple kindnesses and his smile composed his generosity toward God and others. I have never forgotten him.

This simplicity and sacrifice reminds me of the early church. For example, the story of the early church is one of simplicity, sharing, caring, and community.

> All who believed were together and had all things in common. . . . Day by day, as they spent much time together in the temple, they broke bread at home and ate their food with glad and generous hearts, praising God and having the goodwill of all the people. (Acts 2:44, 46-47)

This brief passage offers more than insight into the early church. It is also a call to be people of grace and gratitude, joyous people who, through sharing and simplicity, display God's generosity to the world. I pray we can restore the simple dignity of our own acts.

Throughout the years I have met thousands of people from all walks of life. Regardless of economics, factors like health, family, and happiness seem to be no respecter of persons. I have seen how people create their own joy out of what they have. Gratitude is a common element among people who respect others, exhibit a helpful spirit, and enjoy life. Ungrateful people rarely have these qualities. People with a grateful spirit, no matter their station in life, do not have a harsh or bitter attitude toward others. Those with hearts of gratitude are not mean, small, or apathetic to the plights of others. Gratitude rubs off, and at the end of the day is the one attitude that makes us bigger people and enlarges our influence on others.

A while ago I felt my own gratitude slipping away. I needed to change. So I invited my twenty-one-year-old son to accompany me to a local soup kitchen. Side by side we served the poor and found a new bond as father and son. One of the women there worked in the kitchen most days. When I asked her to share her story, she said, "I make it a point to serve here every week, although, some weeks are more difficult than others. I have other things to do, and I could use my time in other ways. But I come here every week to cook soup because I am grateful. In fact, I don't see how anyone can be a Christian without gratitude!"

Indeed, gratitude makes us whole.

EPILOGUE

I MADE MY PILGRIMAGE ON THE CAMINO DE SANTIAGO during the months I worked on this book. Walking "the Way" changed my outlook on life, renewed my faith, and provided new insights into the myriad ways cherished virtues often get in the way of recognizing God's grace, the amazing depth of God's mercy and blessings.

Walking the Camino, I noted my own excesses. Although I had determined to pack light, I brought too much. Other pilgrims, especially Americans, attempted to prepare for every contingency, bringing enormous backpacks. Some arrived with full pharmacies. Others came with stashes of euros. Still others showed up with fully outfitted tents and camping gear, their pots and pans rattling along the dusty trail.

But as we walked, it was not uncommon to see people leaving their excesses along the Way. In fact, the longer people walked, the more they shed these excessive weights, these cumbersome artifacts of former lives. As we approached Santiago de Compostela— the great cathedral built over the traditional burial site of St. James—it was common to see people leaving behind those vestiges of former lives, sometimes whole backpacks, along the path leading into the city.

But these were merely visible and exterior excesses. The real burdens, the pain, the loss, the grief, the sin, were also being left behind. These interior burdens are what people are trying to deal with when they walk to Camino de Santiago. Most are trying to become more aware of their needs, their motives, their blessings, their spiritual selves. Most are trying to become more aware of God by leaving behind certain trappings or expectations. They are trying to become more immediately aware of God's presence and grace.

I hope you have encountered a new awareness in this book. Perhaps a new awareness of your motives. Perhaps you see the Christian faith through a different set of lenses.

Thank you for taking this brief journey with me and for indulging me as I explored the Christian faith from a different angle, one of self-awareness and deeper introspection. I trust it has been a journey of hope born not just of words or observations, but of a lively discourse in faith, which will transform us in the renewing our minds.

I hope this book elicits additional conversation about the times we live in. Unlike any other time in history, the church is being challenged by the speed of communication and the warp speed of change. It is easy for people of faith to settle for soundbites, tweets, or even casual conversations (and maybe the occasional sermon) instead of delving beneath the surface, which requires more time, more attention, and a greater commitment to dialogue and discernment. We want quick fixes or solutions that, on the surface, seem to be gospel, but on deeper reflection lack grace and godliness.

I hope the church can benefit from considering how the teachings of Jesus not only address our needs but also challenge us to unburden ourselves of false virtues while taking up the cross of Christ, which is joy, hope, love, and salvation.

ACKNOWLEDGMENTS

WHILE WRITING THIS BOOK, I was aware of my own limitations and shortcomings, and gained a deeper appreciation of the myriad ways I am blessed by the virtues and gifts of others. Once again, I thank my wife, Becky, for her graciousness in the fray of notes, for her patience in overlooking my messes, and for providing encouragement, at strategic times, to complete this book. My thanks also extends to the Calvary congregation, to family beyond the circle, and to other spectators and supporters who found this title provocative and engaging.

I am grateful to Helen Lee and to the InterVarsity Press team for their diligent work, and to those first readers who offered feedback on the first draft and helpful comments for improvement. Whatever deficiencies remain I chalk up to my lack, and whatever blessings apply to the IVP staff.

Thanks also to Cynthia Zigmund, my agent. And I also thank those others who came to my rescue by providing feedback and commentary on the manuscript in route. Additional thanks to the many friends who provided illustrations and dialogue (even in anonymity), and to others who have become cherished confidants and colleagues along the way.

FOR REFLECTION AND DISCUSSION

CHAPTER 1—Keeping Your Faith Without Destroying the Faith of Others

1. In what ways can faith become a deadly virtue?

2. What insights have you gained from thinking about faith as a deadly virtue?

3. What, in your estimation, does a mature faith look like or act like?

4. How can our faith become misplaced?

5. How are faith and practice the same? How are they different?

6. How would you describe the Christian faith to another person?

7. What else would you add to your faith? What would you subtract?

8. What do you make of Susie's statement: "I just love Jesus and I want to show it"?

9. How can faith be imperfect but still helpful to us?

10. Hebrews 11:1 describes faith. What would you add to this understanding of faith from your own experience?

CHAPTER 2—From Loving Our Way to God's Way of Love

1. Why do you think different nuances of love are expressed in the Bible?

2. Why is love so elusive in our world?

3. Why was Leo Buscaglia's love class was so popular?

4. Is it possible the expression "Hate the sin, but love the sinner" is incomplete? How?

5. How might the scriptural references to love in the Gospel of John and in 1-2 John be helpful in understanding how we should live out our faith?

6. How might the church have a renewal of love?

7. What do you think are the deepest needs in the world today? How can love address these needs?

8. How can love as a deadly virtue be transformed into *agapē* love?

9. How do you define *love*?

10. What do you make of the old maxim "The love in your heart is not here to stay, it is not love until you give it away"?

CHAPTER 3—From Focusing on Our Family to Seeing God's Family First

1. What do you make of the phrase "Christian family"?

2. How does Jesus press the boundaries of our definition of family?

3. How have you experienced the church as a family? How not?

4. How does being "in Christ" redefine the concept of family?

5. Read Galatians 3:28. What insights about the family can be found here?

6. What do you think are the largest challenges being experienced by families today?

7. What communities have you witnessed that have helped you define family?

8. What do you make of the phrase "breakdown of the family," and what do you think these breakdowns are?

9. Do you have a spiritual genealogy? What is it?

10. How might we redefine church family in light of Christ's teachings?

CHAPTER 4—The Power of One or the Power of the One

1. What is most frightening about power?

2. How are strength and power the same? How do they differ?

3. In what ways is God's power made known in weakness rather than in our strength?

4. How does our modern infatuation with competition add or detract from our concepts of power?

5. What do you think are some differences between a boss and a leader?

6. How is power misused today? In society? In the church? In politics? In the association of the church with politics?

7. How does the church provide power in healthy ways? In unhealthy ways?

8. Where do you see power struggles in the world? In the workplace? At school? At home? In society?

9. What are some powers that have been misused by people of faith?

10. How are prayer and strength related?

CHAPTER 5—The Lure of Success or the Allure of Grace

1. Why do you think happiness is so elusive?

2. What do you make of the saying "Do not pray for an easy life; pray to be a strong person"?

3. If you could make a list of happy moments in your life, what would it include?

4. Who are the happiest people you know? What do you think makes them happy?

5. What are some other words for happiness?

6. How is blessing different from happiness?

7. How is joy different from happiness?

8. What are some experiences that make you happy?

9. Where do you see definitions of happiness in the Bible?

10. What makes you happy (in light of this chapter)?

CHAPTER 6—When Good Isn't Good Enough, God Is Still Good

1. How do you interpret Jesus' words in Mark 10:17-18?

2. How do you define *goodness*?

3. Is it possible for goodness and pride to be related? How?

4. How might faith and goodness be confused? How are they sometimes used interchangeably?

5. Can doing good to others sometimes produce bad results? Explain.

6. What are some evidences that you see in our world that goodness is still prevalent?

7. How are goodness and grace related?

8. Why do you think the Bible contains so many stories about flawed people?

9. How can goodness become a deadly virtue?

10. How have you experienced goodness in your life?

CHAPTER 7—Generous to a Fault or Overflowing with Gratitude

1. How do you see the tension between generosity and pride?

2. Do you think church leaders exploit generosity? If so, how?

3. How would you define *generosity* (as a tithe, as something else, as more)?

4. Is it possible for generosity to be misplaced? Explain.

5. How can we practice generosity beyond our financial gifts?

6. What do you make of the phrase "attitude of gratitude"?

7. What do you think of Martin Luther's idea of the three stages of conversion (the mind, the heart, the purse)?

8. What makes generosity difficult?

9. Who are some of the most generous people you have known? What made them generous?

10. How can the church show more generosity in our communities?

Additional Questions

1. What are the most challenging deadly virtues explored in this book?

2. How does the concept of deadly virtues impact your concept of faith?

3. What other deadly virtues might you add to a list?

4. How do deadly virtues differ from the seven deadly sins? How might they be similar?

5. What are some of the greatest challenges you believe the church is facing today? How can dialogue on the deadly virtues affect these challenges?

NOTES

INTRODUCTION

[1]John Chrysostom, Homily 1, *The Works of St. Chrysostom*, Select Library of the Nicene and Post-Nicene Fathers of the Christian Church, ed. Philip Schaff (Buffalo, NY: Christian Literature Publishing, 1889), 9:342.

[2]John Scotus, quoted in Henry Bett, *Johannes Scotus Erigena* (Cambridge: Cambridge University Press, 1925).

1 KEEPING YOUR FAITH WITHOUT DESTROYING THE FAITH OF OTHERS

[1]Pope Francis, "Letter to a Non-Believer," *Vatican*, September 4, 2013, http://w2.vatican.va/content/francesco/en/letters/2013/documents /papa-francesco_20130911_eugenio-scalfari.html. In this letter, Pope Francis responds to Dr. Eugenio Scalfari, journalist of the Italian newspaper *La Repubblica*.

2 FROM LOVING OUR WAY TO GOD'S WAY OF LOVE

[1]C. S. Lewis, *The Four Loves* (New York: Harcourt, Brace, 1960), 139.

[2]This is a traditional Jewish parable that I have heard over the years. I cannot find the source, so I believe it is anonymous.

[3]Wesley's rules, and the General Rules of the Methodist Church, are found in the *Discipline of the United Methodist Church* (Nashville: United Methodist Publishing House, 2016). See also www.umc.org/what-we-believe /general-rules-of-the-methodist-church.

[4]Based on a parable of Søren Kierkegaard's in Todd Outcalt, *Candles in the Dark* (Hoboken, NJ: John Wiley, 2002), 80.

[5]This parable is the author's adaptation from the *Patrologia Graeca*.

[6]Mother Teresa, quoted in "Mother Teresa Quotes," Goodreads, accessed September 20, 2016, www.goodreads.com/author/quotes/838305 .Mother_Teresa.

3 From Focusing on Our Family to Seeing God's Family First

[1]Augustine, *Confessions*, ed. Philip Schaff, trans. J. G. Pilkington, Nicene and Post-Nicene Fathers, first series, vol. 1 (Buffalo, NY: Christian Literature Publishing, 1887), chap. 1.

[2]This parable is the author's adaptation from the *Patrologia Graeca*.

4 The Power of One or the Power of the One

[1]Joyce Kilmer, "Trees," 1913.

[2]Dietrich Bonhoeffer, *Life Together* (New York: Harper & Row, 1954), 21.

[3]Ibid., 27.

[4]Raphael Brown, *The Little Flowers of St. Francis* (New York: Doubleday, 1971), 72-74.

[5]Martin Luther, quoted in *The Westminster Collection of Christian Quotations*, ed. Martin H. Manser (Louisville, KY: Westminster John Knox, 2001), 211.

[6]Martin Luther, "Life Quotes from Martin Luther on His Birthday, November 10, 1483," Lutherans for Life, November 10, 2013, www.lutheransforlife.org/article /life-quotes-from-martin-luther-on-his-birthday-november-10-1483.

6 When Good Isn't Good Enough, God Is Still Good

[1]Tracy Connor, Hannah Rappleye, and Erika Angulo, "What Does Haiti Have to Show for $13 Billion in Earthquake Aid?," NBC News, January 12, 2015, www.nbcnews.com/news/investigations/what-does-haiti-have-show-13 -billion-earthquake-aid-n281661.

[2]"Aid in Haiti," Haiti Net, accessed September 20, 2016, www.northeastern .edu/haitinet/aid-in-haiti.

7 Generous to a Fault or Overflowing with Gratitude

[1]While Methodists use this quote widely, and it is commonly known as "Wesley's rule," it is actually a compilation of quotes.